Play It!

LEVEL 2

A Superfast Way to Learn Awesome Songs on Your Piano or Keyboard

CHILDREN'S SONGS

By Jennifer Kemmeter and Antimo Marrone

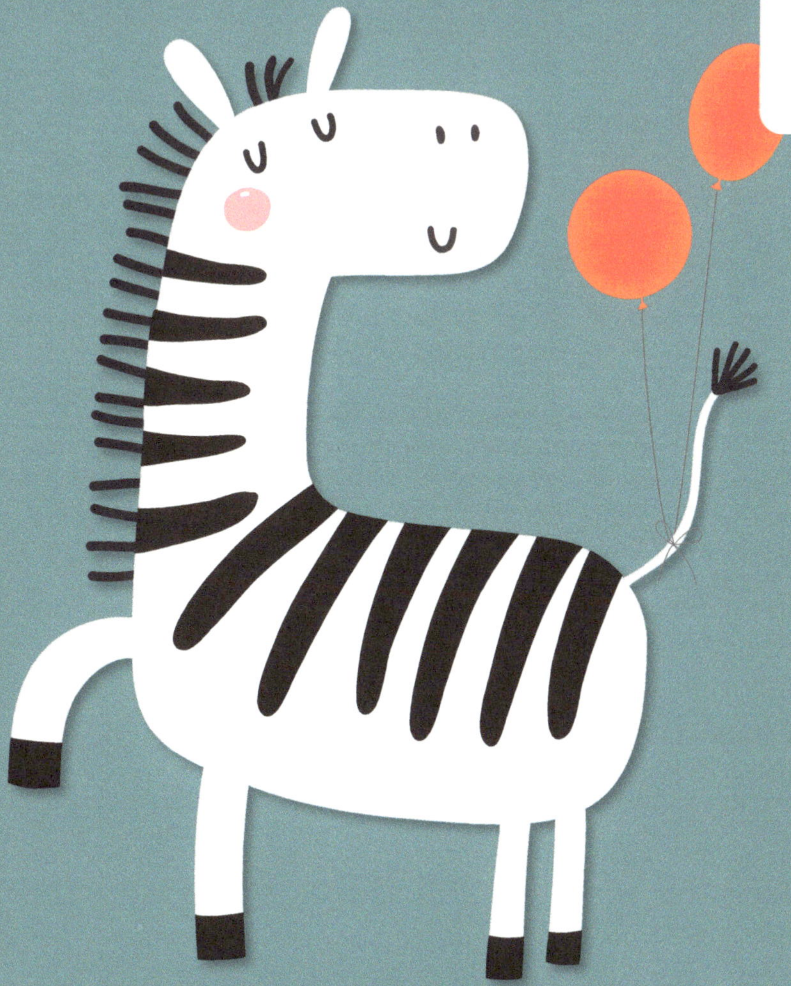

Turner Publishing Company
Nashville, Tennessee
www.turnerpublishing.com

Play It! Children's Songs for Piano (Level 2)

Library of Congress Control Number: 2026932610

ISBN: 9781513142029 (paperback) | 9781513142036 (hardback) | 9781513142043 (ebook)

Published by Graphic Arts Books
an imprint of West Margin Press

WestMarginPress.com

jenniferkemmeter.com

0 1 2 3 4 5 6 7 8 9

Contents

Hi Kids! My Name is Zooey. I'm going to teach you how to play music. Using my awesome system, you don't need to know anything fancy or technical—all you need is to know your colors, be able to follow a tune, and maybe even sing along. It's easy! Once you learn my cool, color-coded system, you'll be able to play a bunch of songs you probably already recognize, just by pressing the colors on the keyboard. Let's play!

Unsure what a song should sound like? Don't worry! We've collected all the songs in one place so you can listen to them!

Just scan this QR code, and any time you see this symbol:

find the corresponding letter or number and hit "download" to hear the song!

1
2
3
4
5
6
7

Good Piano Posture
also known as The Pro's Pose!

It may not seem important at first, but when you sit down to play, the way you sit on the bench or chair plays a part in how good your music sounds.

Follow this diagram to look and sound like a pro:

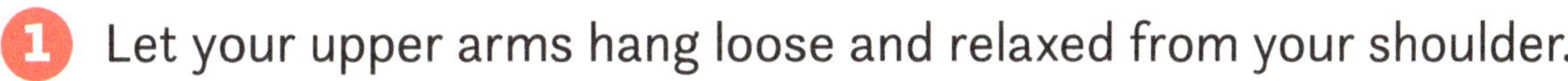

1. Let your upper arms hang loose and relaxed from your shoulder.
2. Keep your back straight and lean forward slightly.
3. You want your elbows slightly higher than the keyboard to get the best sound from the keys (you may need to adjust the seat height or sit on a book to get things just right).
4. Sit on the front half of the bench or chair so that your weight is positioned forward toward the keyboard.
5. Position yourself so that your knees are slightly underneath the keyboard.
6. Keep your feet flat on the floor. If they don't touch, put some books or a step underneath them.
7. Use rounded hands to strike the keys—hold your wrists above the keyboard and arch your fingers down toward the keys.

That's it! Now you look like a rock star!

How to Use This Book

Now that you look cool at the keyboard, you're just five steps away from playing your first song! Here's how:

1. **Cut out the color-coded labels** on page 69 or 71. Be sure to set aside the red "Middle C" label, because this one is special. The letters on the labels represent the musical notes on the keyboard. So, red labels represent C notes in music; yellow labels represent E notes; blue labels represent G notes; et cetera.

   TIP: To make the labels last longer, ask your parent or teacher to laminate the sheet of labels before cutting them.

2. **Attach the "Middle C" label to the keyboard.** It's the one nearest the center of the keyboard that's shaped like an "L". You can use tape or removable blue putty to secure the label.

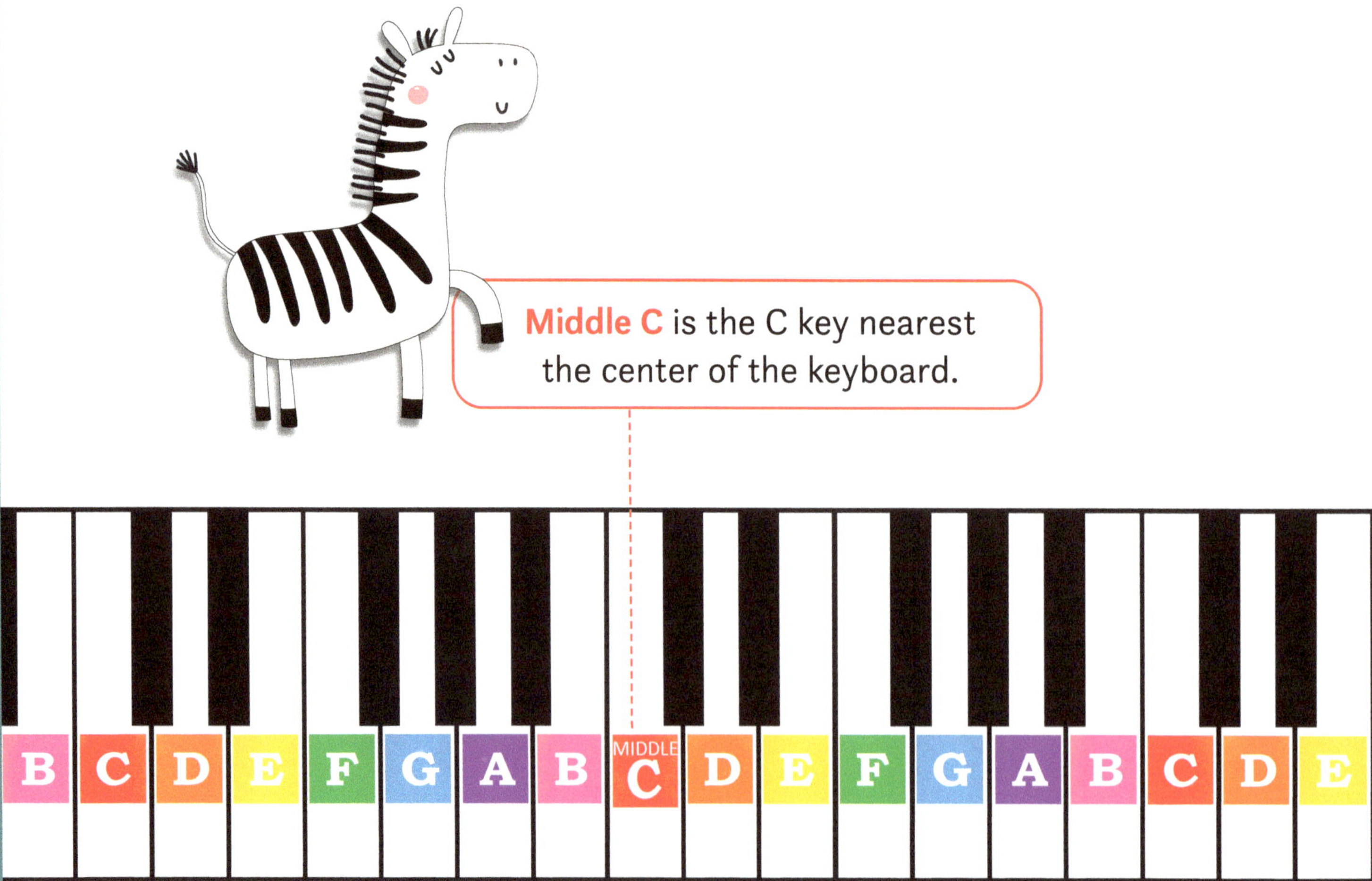

3. Once you have attached the Middle C, **follow the diagram** on the top of the pages for the song you want to play to attach the rest of the color-coded labels.

   TIP: Put any loose labels into a covered container and tuck them into a drawer or your piano bench for storage.

4. Again referring to the diagram, **place your hands in the correct position** for playing the song. Starting position of your hands is shown at the top of each page. The notes you will play are shown on the keyboard. Hand position, the key for the left-most finger, is shown on the shirtcuff.

   Then, shift your attention to the song and begin to play, pressing the keys with the colors and using the correct finger as shown.

Twinkle, Twinkle Little Star

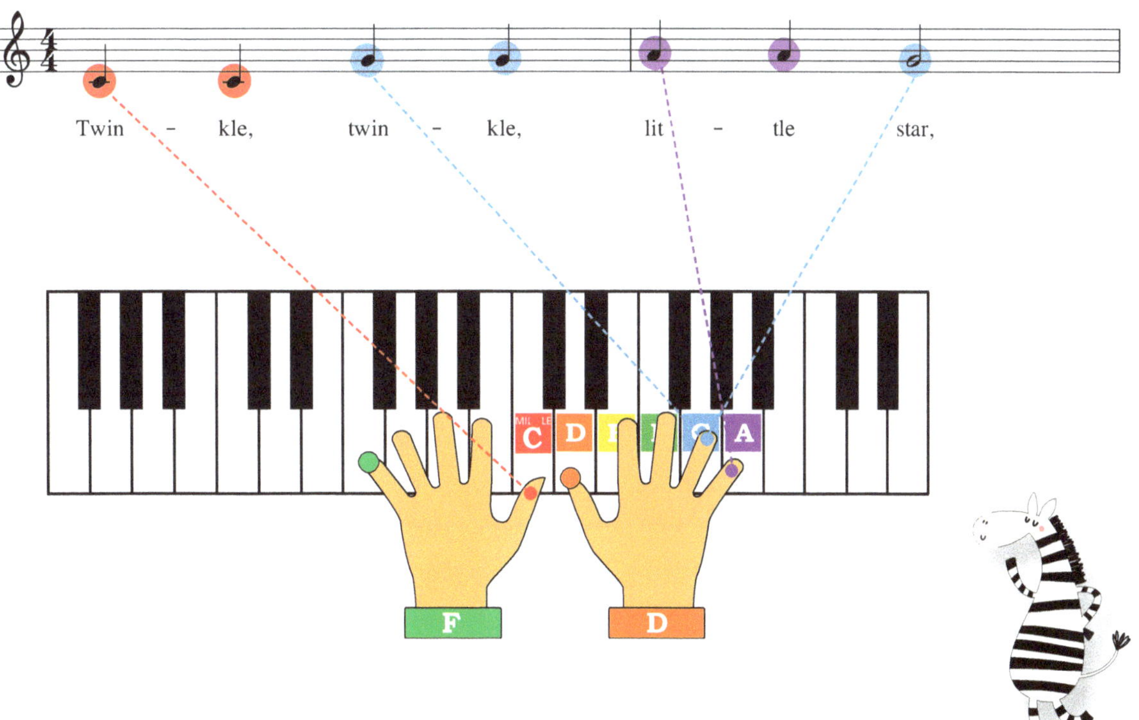

5. **Have fun!** Once you get the hang of it, you'll be able to play a ton of new songs. Look for me throughout the book—I'll be giving you extra tips and tricks so you'll become even more of a rock star as you go.

Let's Get Started!

Welcome to Level 2 piano! Now you're ready to play songs where your right and left hands will play at the same time. The right hand plays the melody, while the left plays a harmony.

Each hand has its own staff of music: the bass clef for the left hand and the treble clef for the right hand.

They are connected by one ledger line between them, where Middle C is the bridge between them.

The middle of the treble clef curls around the G line:

The dots of the bass clef are on either side of the F line:

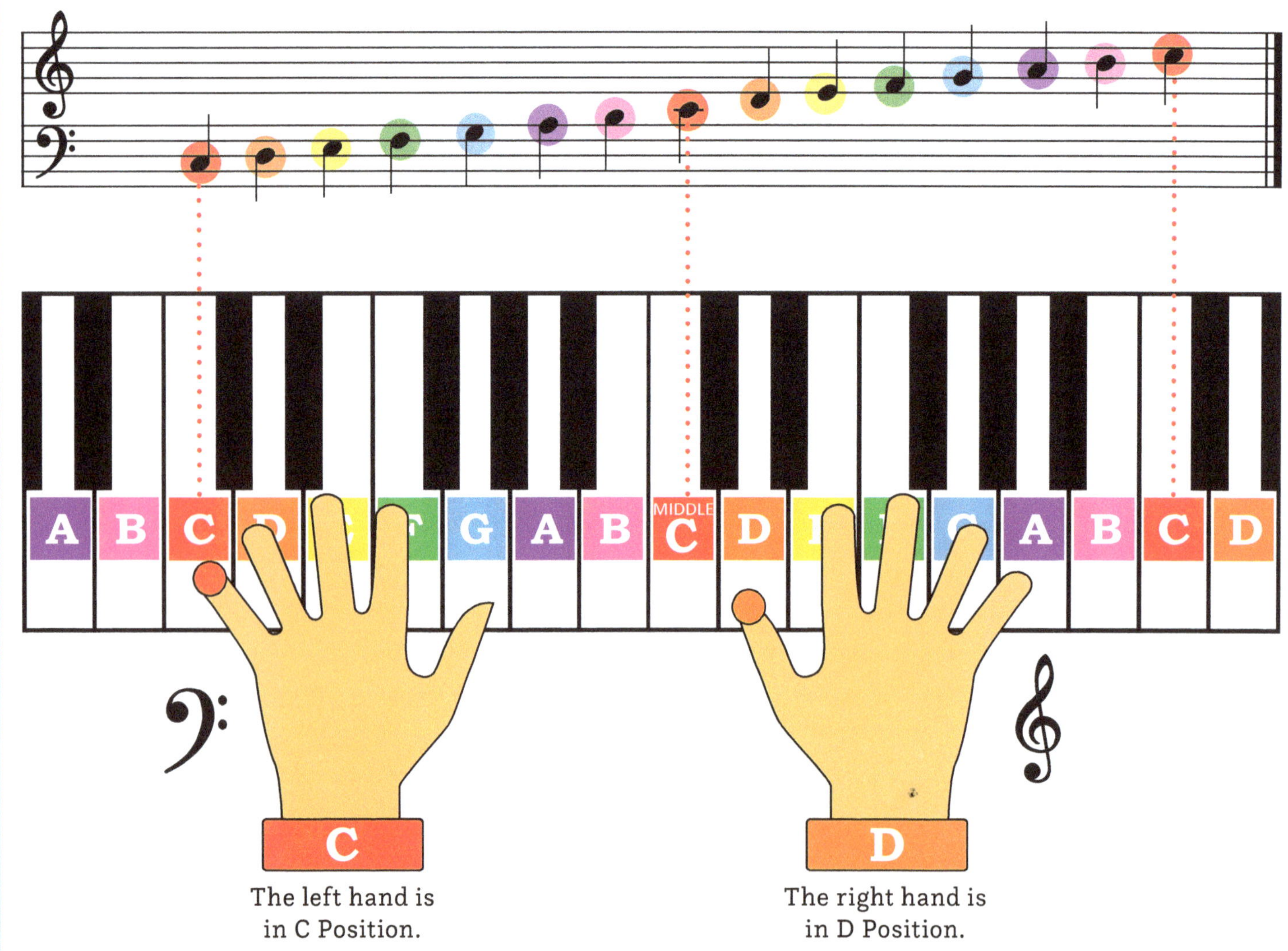

The left hand is in C Position.

The right hand is in D Position.

Hand and Finger Positions

When setting your hands to play, curve the fingers of both hands as if you were gently holding a ball. All fingers are now nearly the same length, and the thumb is in playing position on its side.

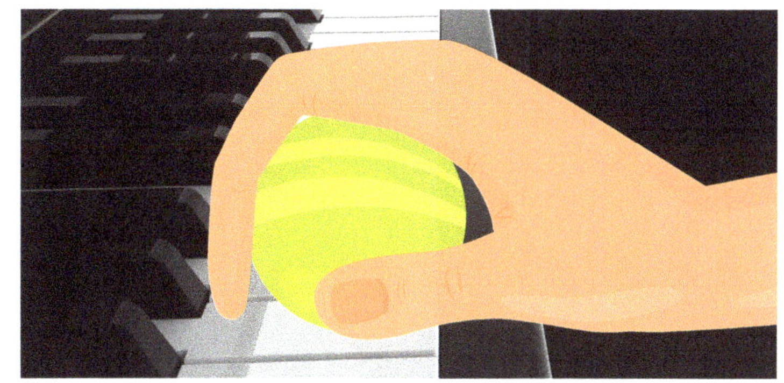

Your hands will be much more active in this book! Here are some moves you will master:

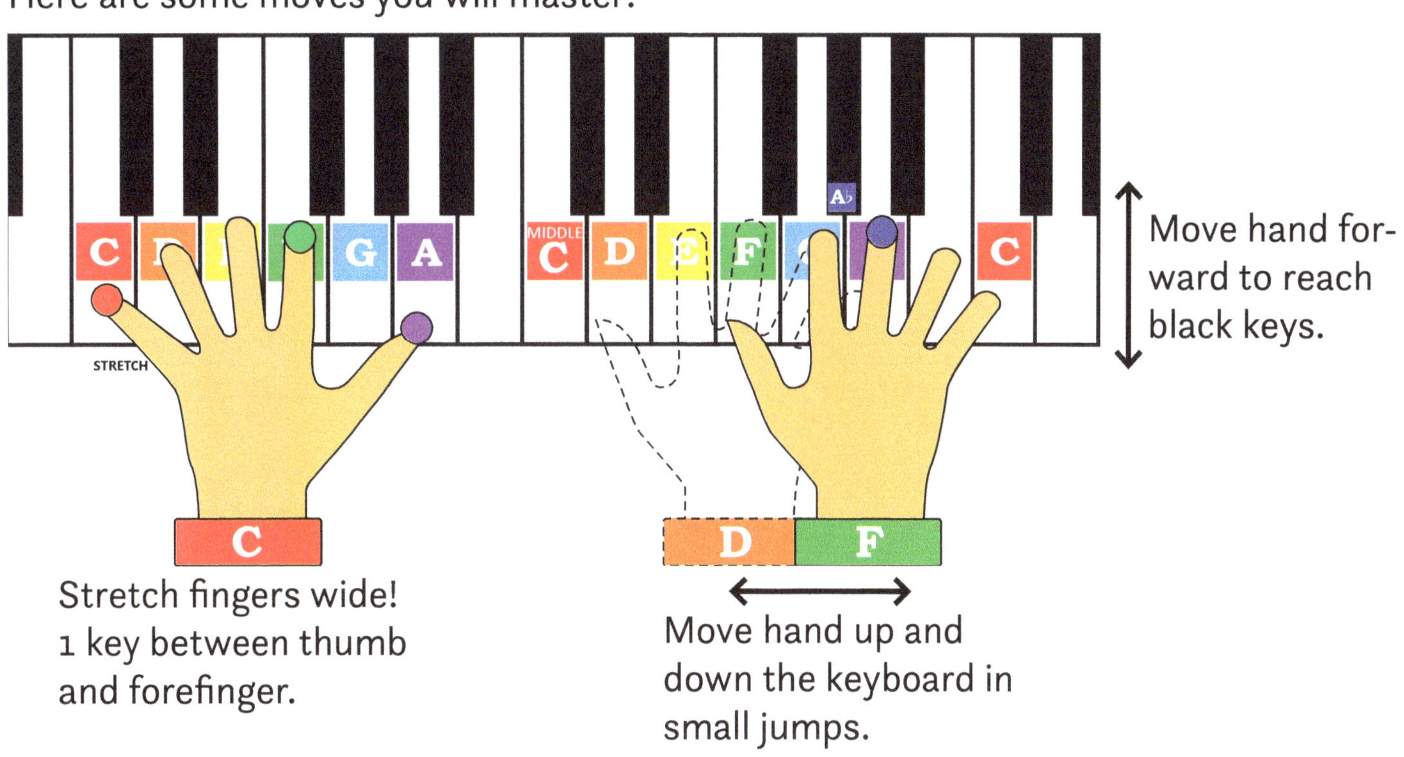

Move hand forward to reach black keys.

Stretch fingers wide! 1 key between thumb and forefinger.

Move hand up and down the keyboard in small jumps.

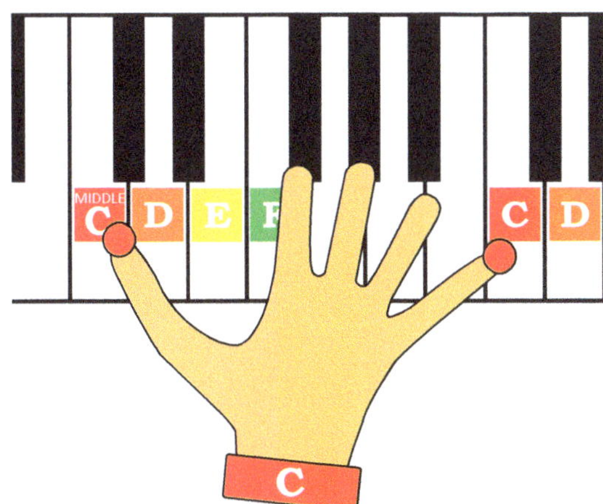

Stretch fingers wider! Play wide 7- and 8-key arpeggios, and octaves with the same hand.

Walk fingers 2 and 3 over the thumb in cross-overs.

Hand and Finger Diagrams

Starting position of your hands is shown at the top of each page. The notes you will play are shown on the keyboard. Hand position, the key for the left-most finger, is shown on the shirt cuff. Warm up by playing up and down the notes in starting position.

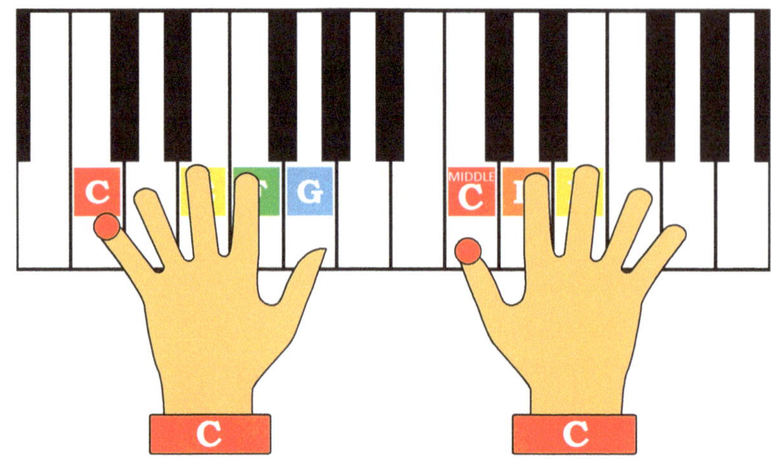

Finger Crossovers

Fingers 2 and 3 sometimes walk over the thumb in a cross-over (page 39). Fingers numbers are shown below.

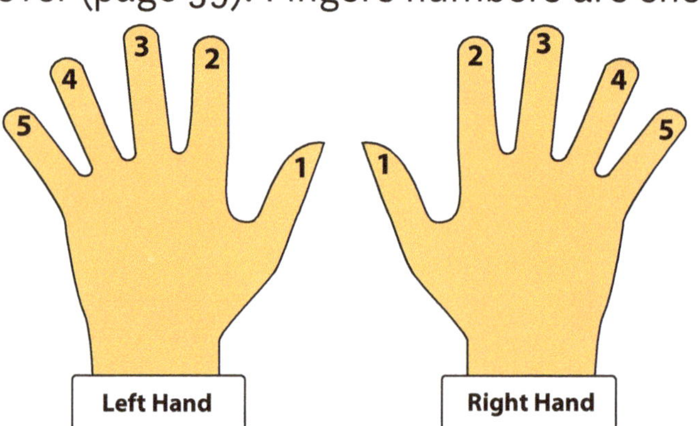

Finger Bubbles

Hand diagrams with colored finger bubbles show you which fingers to play the next few notes with. The hand stays there until a new position is shown. The hand position is shown on the cuff!

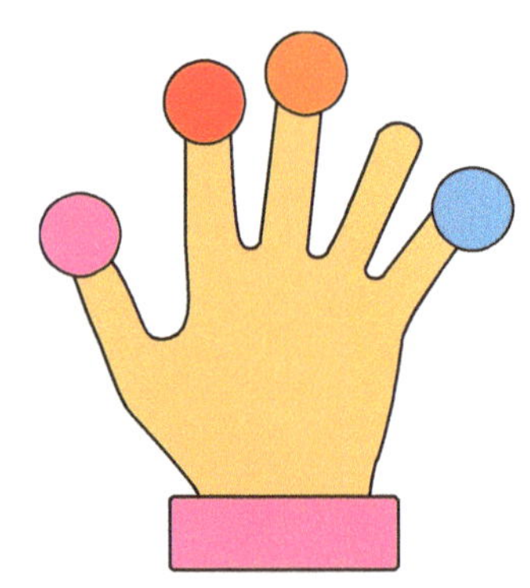

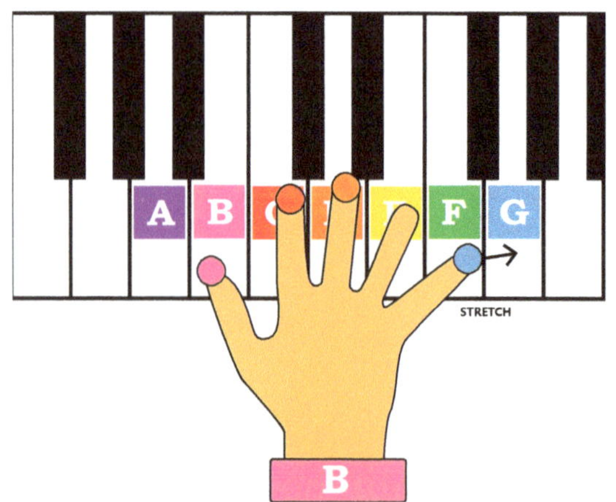

Clefs, Time Signature, and Measures

The **Clef** at the start of the song tells you what pitch of notes to play—high or low—with left or right hand. **Time Signature** tells you how to count time. The top number tells you how many beats are in a measure. The number below it tells you what kind of note gets one beat. The **G clef** at left tells you to play high notes with the right hand, the **4/4** time signature tells us there are 4 beats in a measure, and a quarter note gets one beat.

The musical staff is divided by vertical bar lines. The space between a pair of bar lines is called a measure. This is a unit of time, made up of a number of beats, shown in the top number of the time signature.

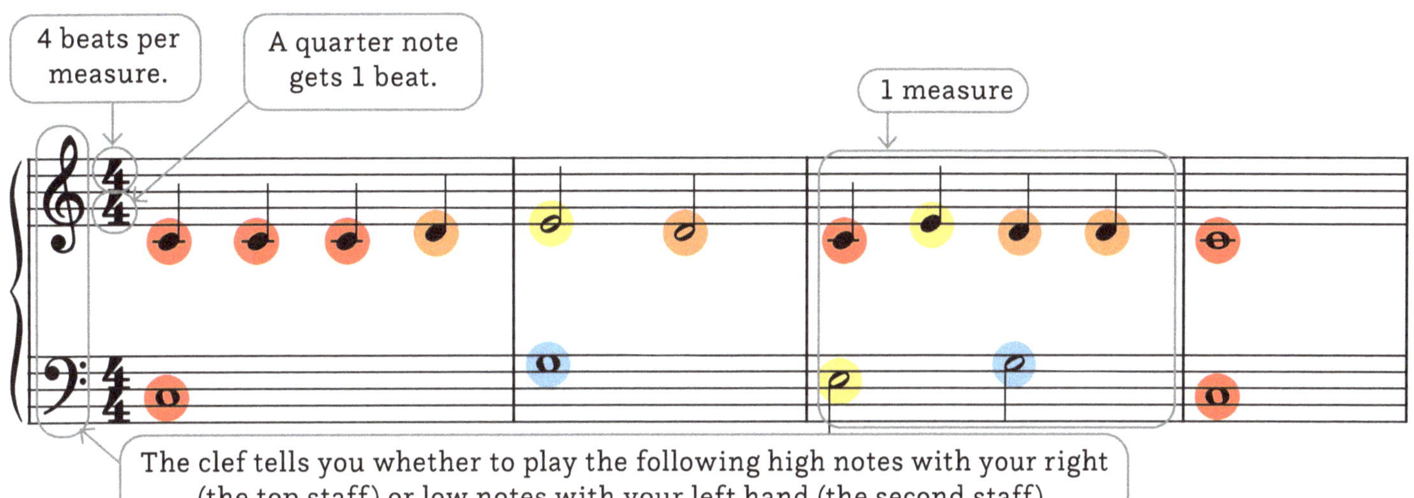

Notes and Rests

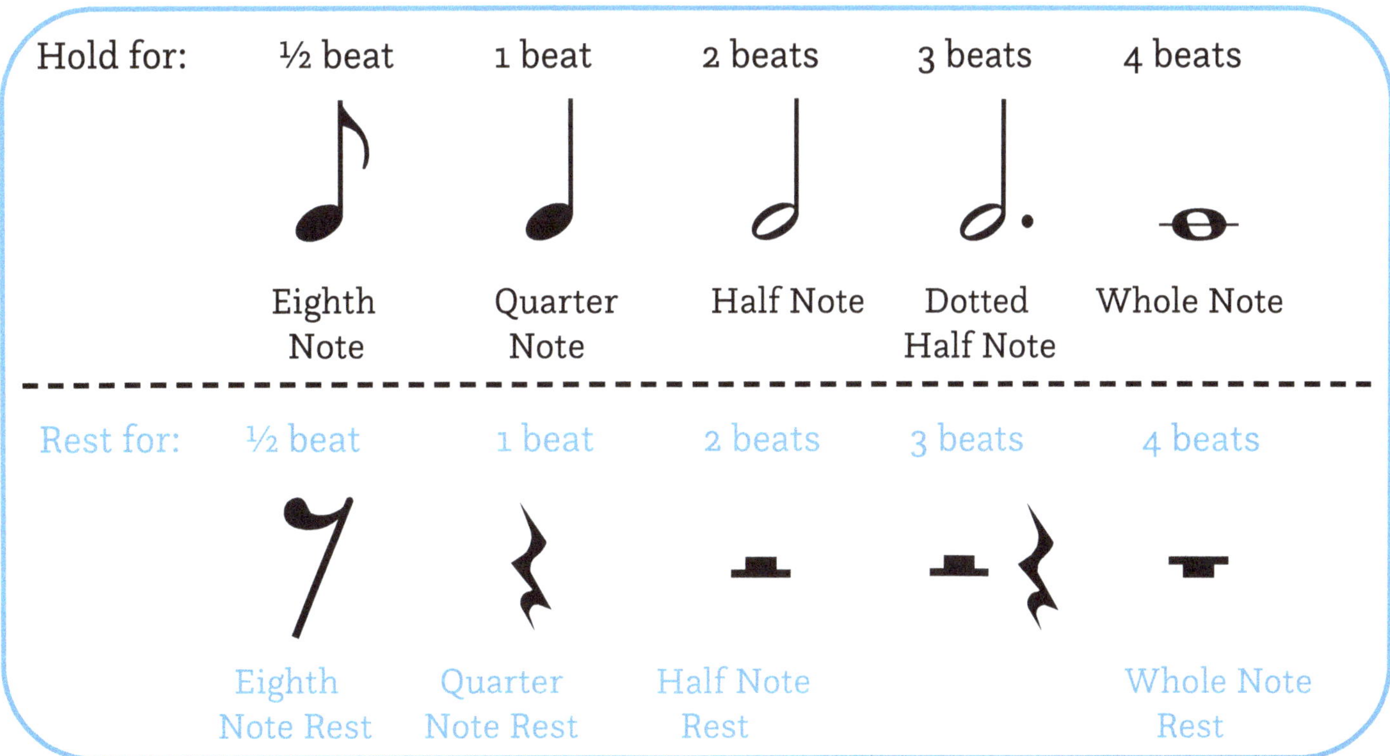

Warming Up to Play a Two-Part Song

Follow this approach for every song you attempt:

1. Play the 5-note warm ups like those shown on the next page, from the right hand's first position. Say the name of each note aloud as you play.
2. Play the 5-note warm ups from the left hand's first position. Again, say the names of the notes aloud. (Turn the page for the next step!)
3. Play the song 5–10 times with the RIGHT HAND ONLY to learn that part of the song. The left hand should not play at all.
4. Play the song 5–10 times with the LEFT HAND ONLY to learn that part of the song. The right hand should not play at all.
5. Slowly play the parts of both hands together at the same time. When your note and timing accuracy is strong, play to a normal tempo. Listen to the song audio and use the metronome on our website to keep time and build to the right tempo.

Warming Up: Sample from C Position

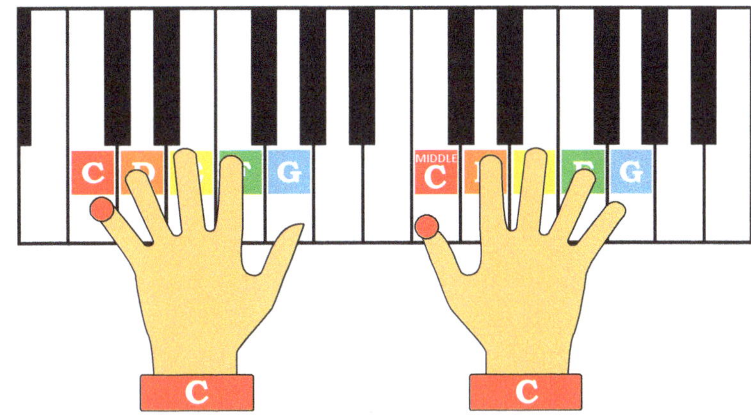

1. Right hand warm up

2. Left hand warm up

Turn the page for steps 3, 4, and 5.

Exercise 1: Learn to Play Each Hand Individually

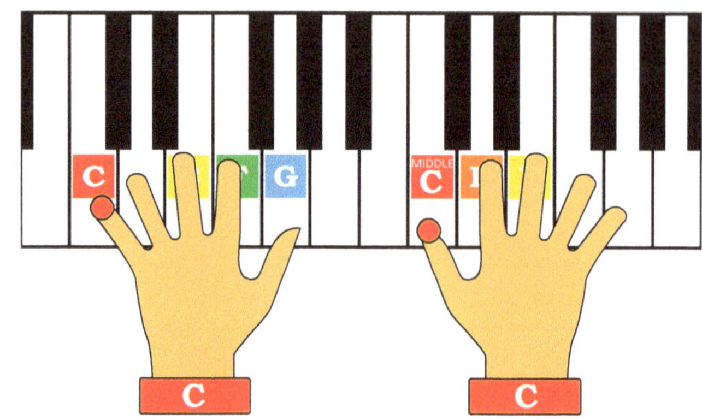

3. First play only the right hand part (the melody).

4. Then practice only the left hand (the harmony).

5. Play both parts together.

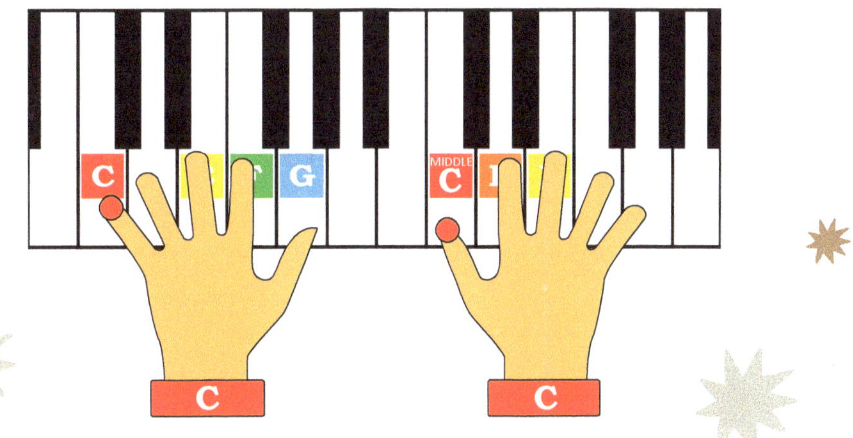

1. Au Clair de la Lune

Follow this approach to learn every new song!

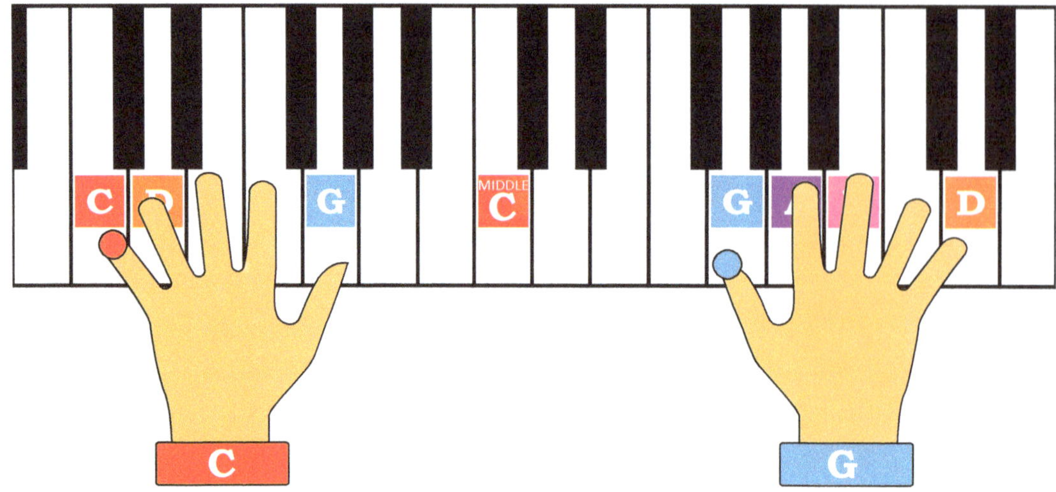

2. Merrily We Roll Along

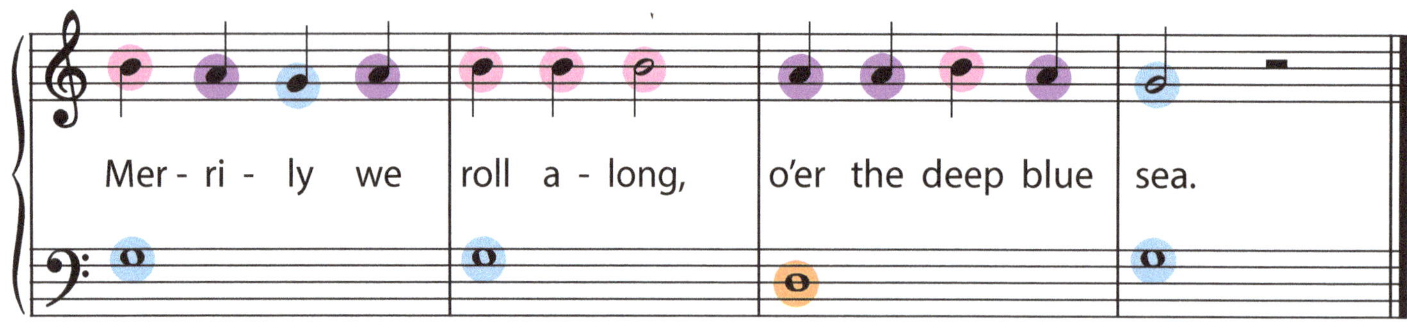

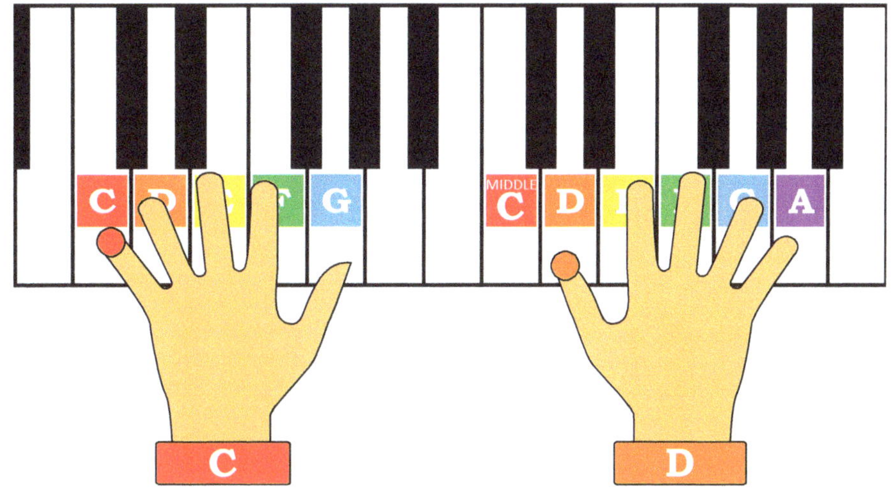

3. A Tisket, A Tasket

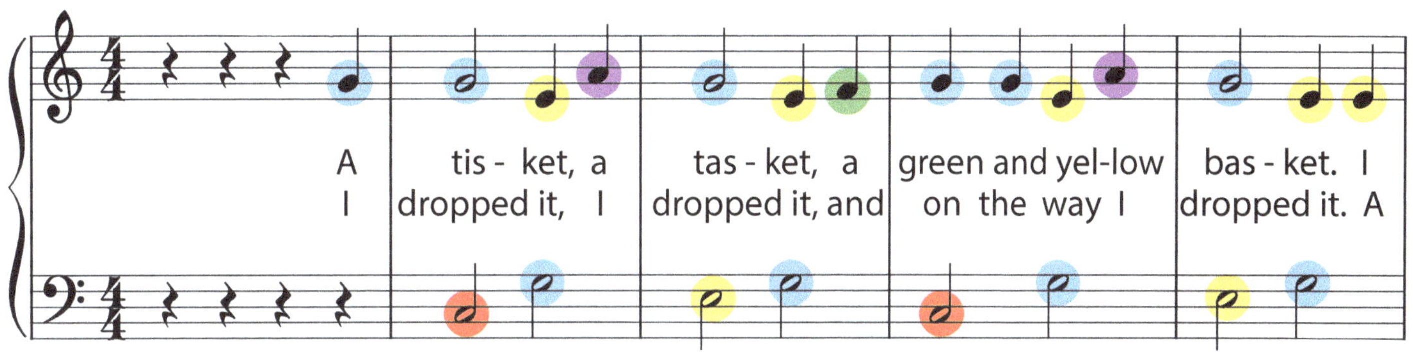

Change to new position shown.

Exercise 2: The 6-Key Arpeggio

Time to stretch your fingers out of base position! Stretch the thumb to the next key over, leaving a key between fingers 1 and 2. This will allow you to play 6 keys with 5 fingers, while keeping your hand in the same position!

Left Hand: Base Position

Left Hand: Stretch Position

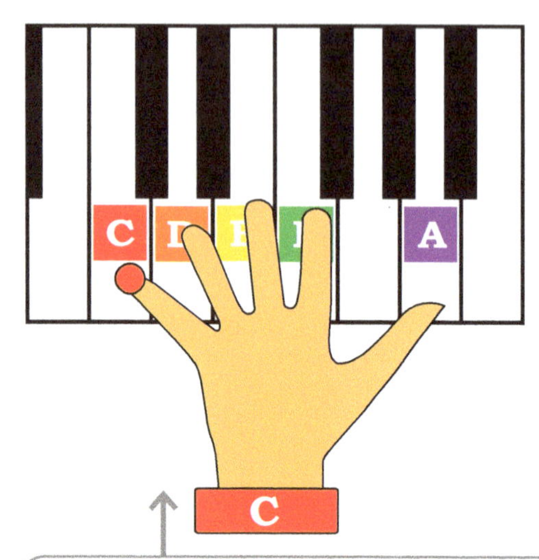

You may find it more comfortable to move your hand forward slightly as you stretch to new keys.

A. Play Left Hand in Base Position

B. Play Left Hand in Stretch Position

C. Alternate between fingers in base and stretch positions

Be ready to move your thumb between base and stretch!

Now try the same exercises with your right hand. Remember the gap is between the thumb and first finger.

Right Hand: Base Position

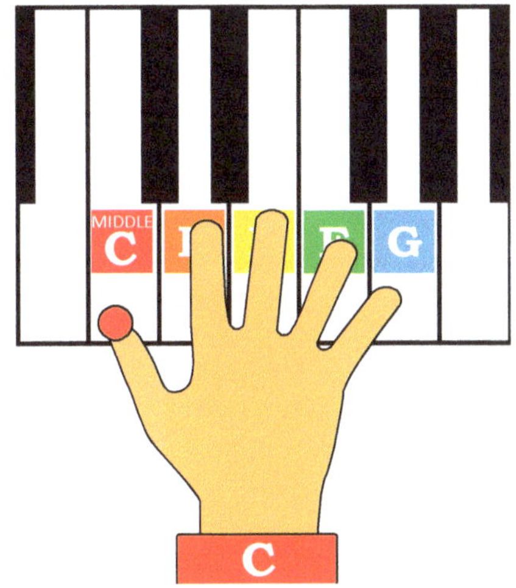

Right Hand: Stretch Position

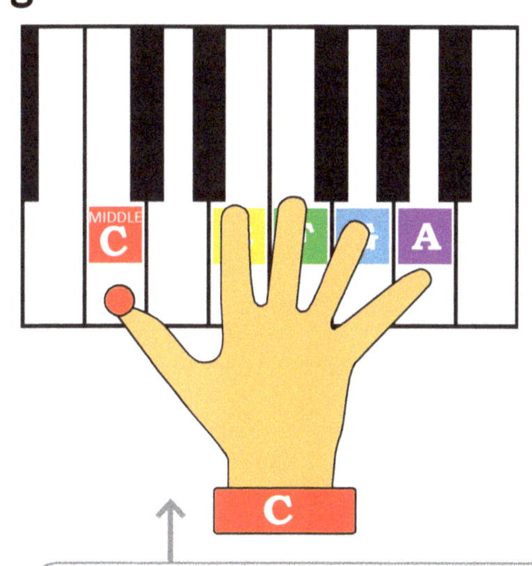

You may find it more comfortable to move your hand forward slightly as you stretch to new keys.

A. Play Right Hand in Base Position

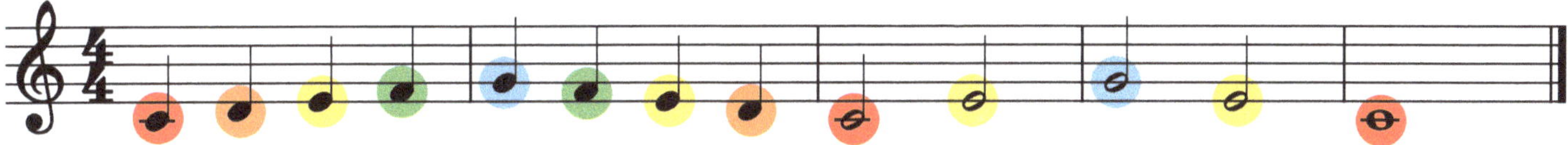

B. Play Right Hand in Stretch Position

C. Alternate between fingers in base and stretch positions

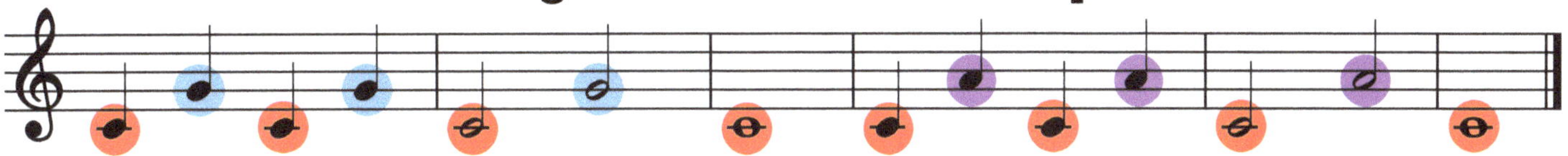

Be ready to move between base and stretch positions!

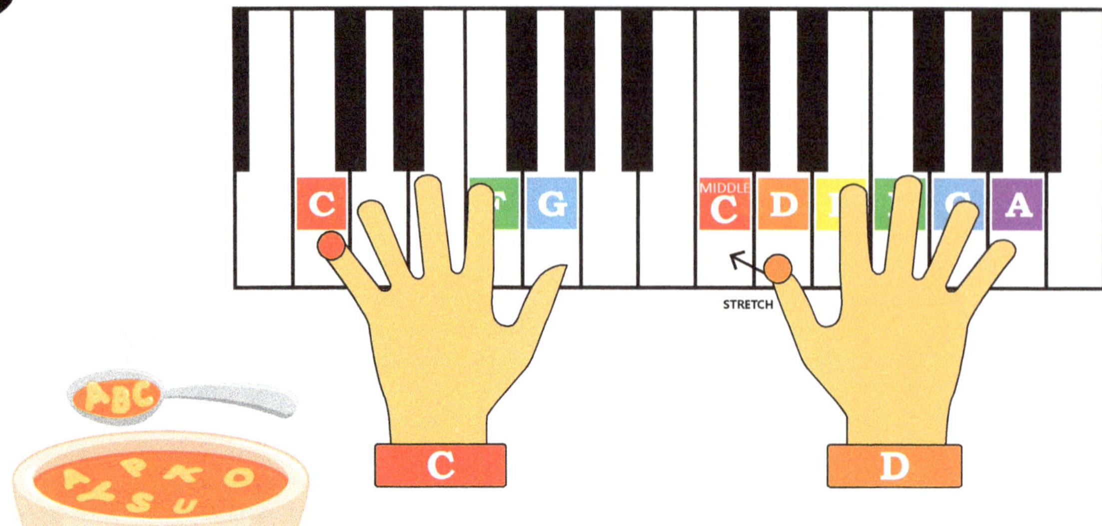

4. Alphabet Song

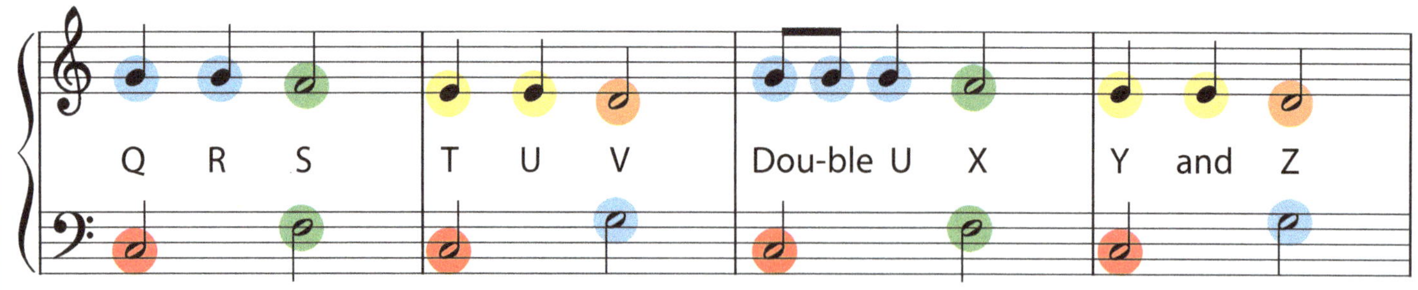

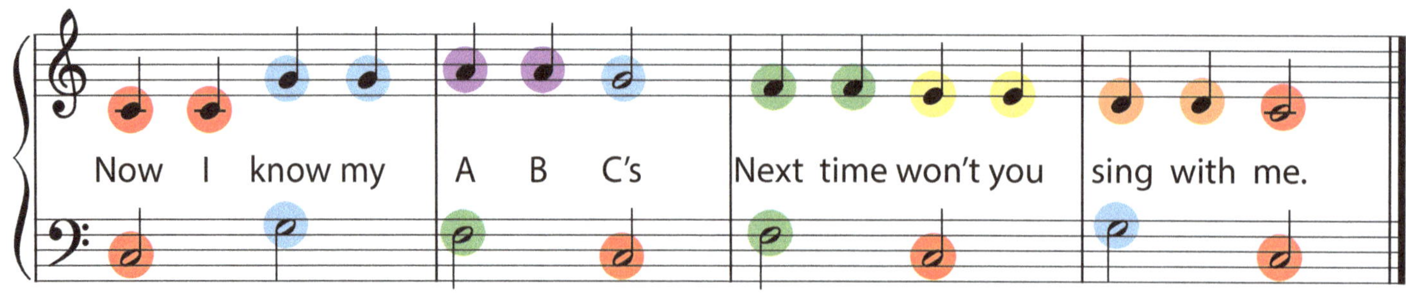

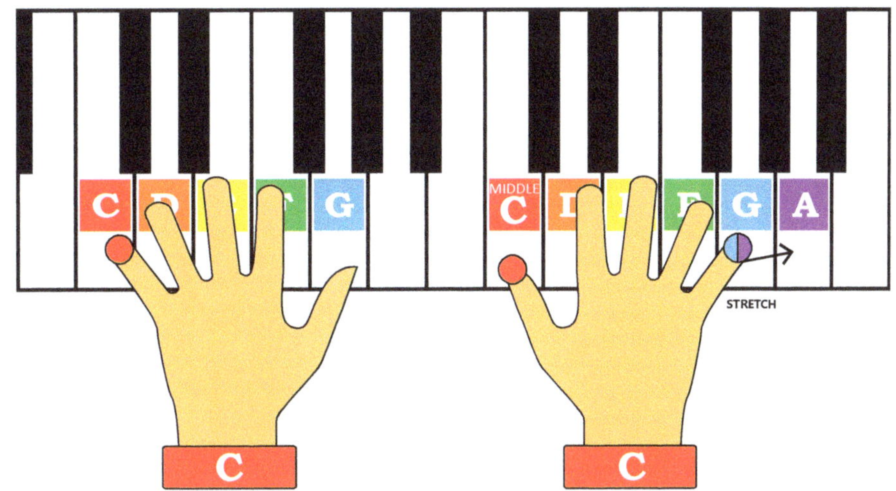

5. Lavender's Blue

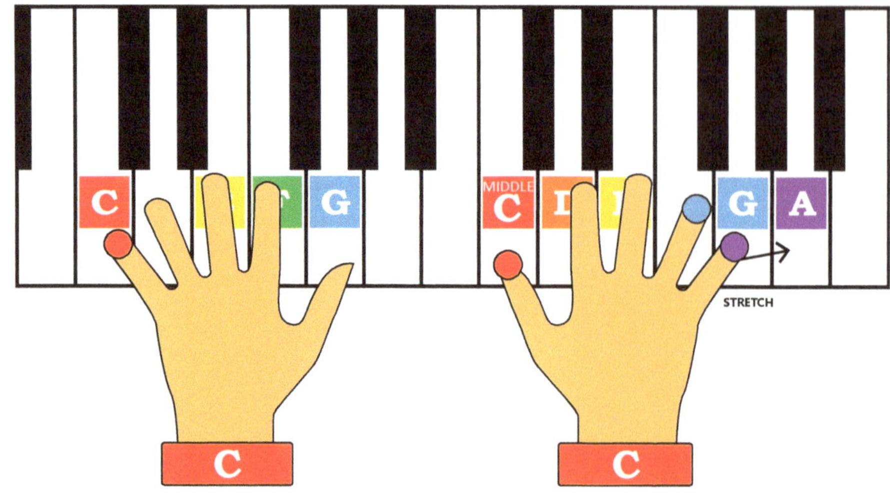

6. The Farmer in the Dell

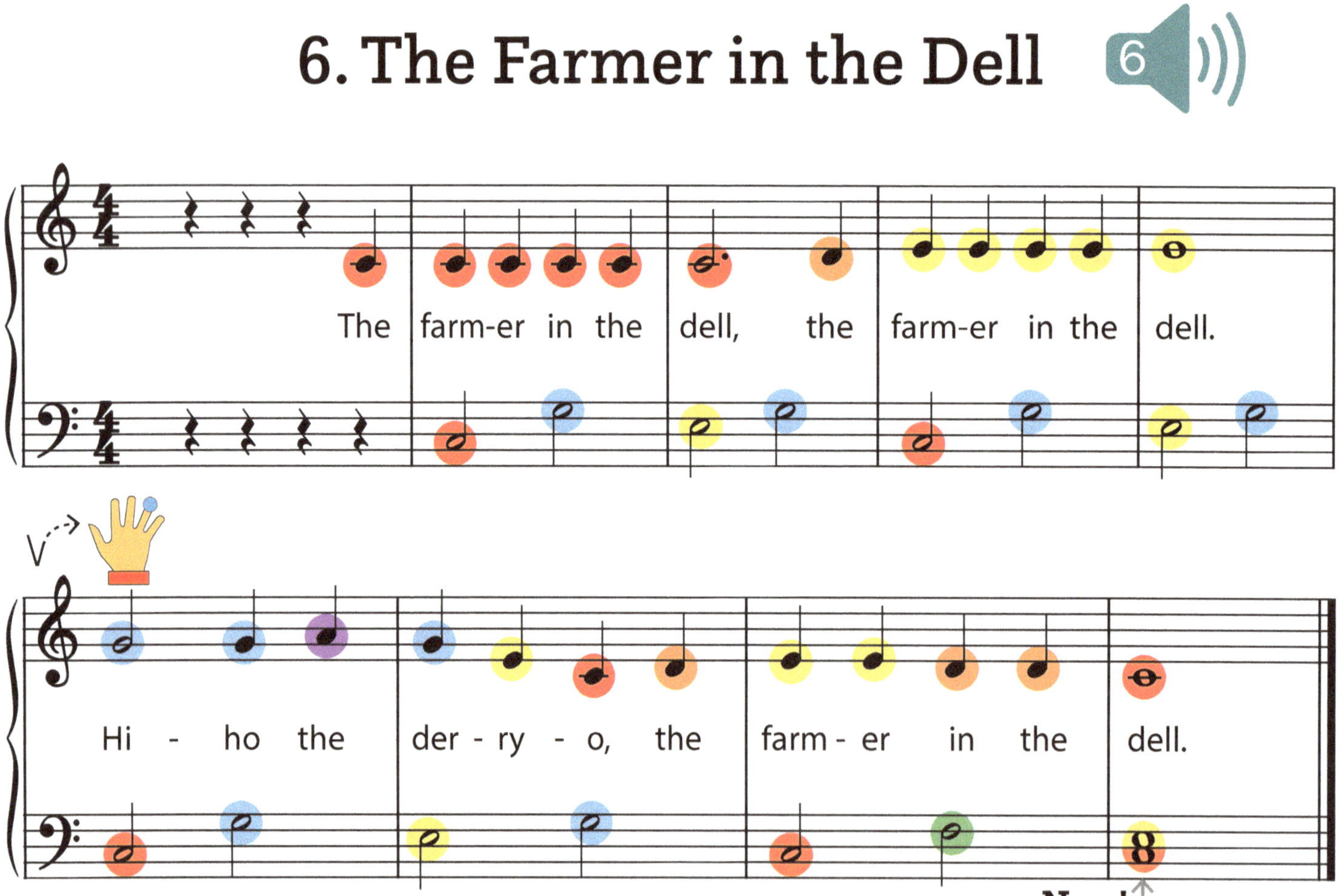

The farm-er in the dell, the farm-er in the dell.

Hi - ho the der - ry - o, the farm - er in the dell.

New! The hand makes a small jump in the direction shown.

New! Notes stacked vertically are played at the same time.

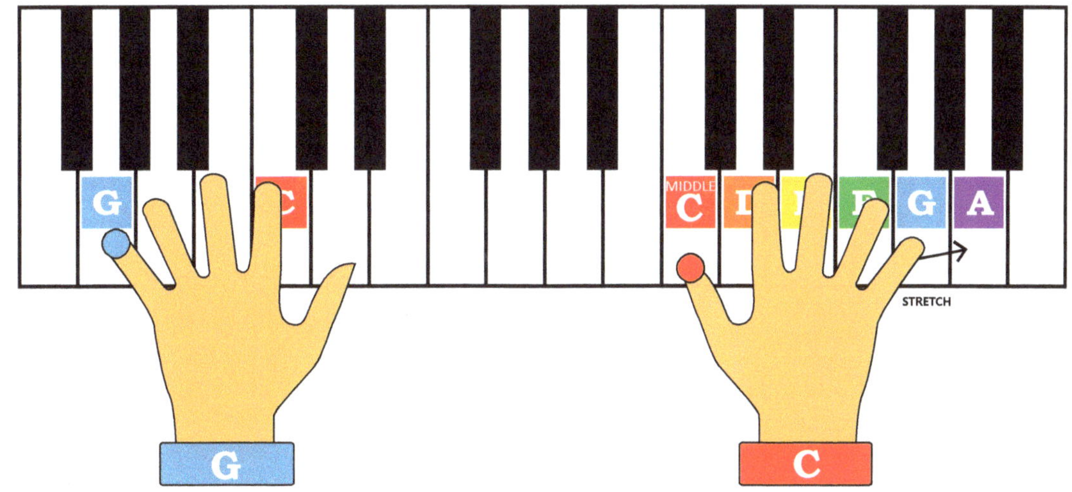

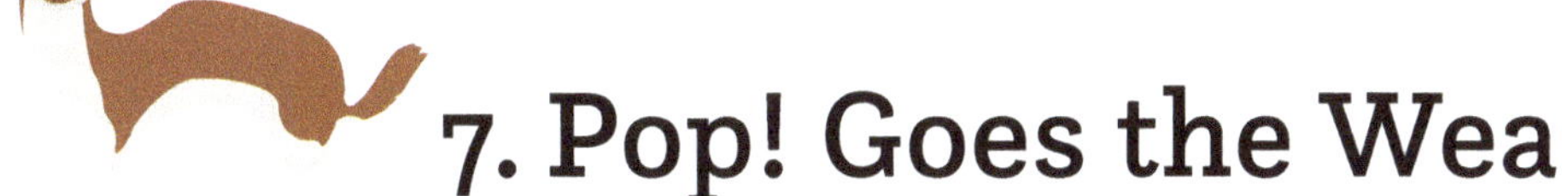

7. Pop! Goes the Weasel

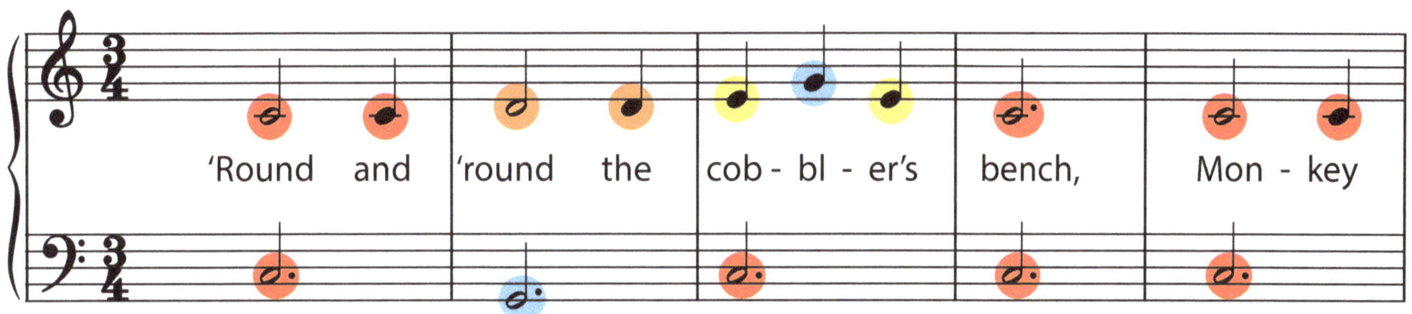

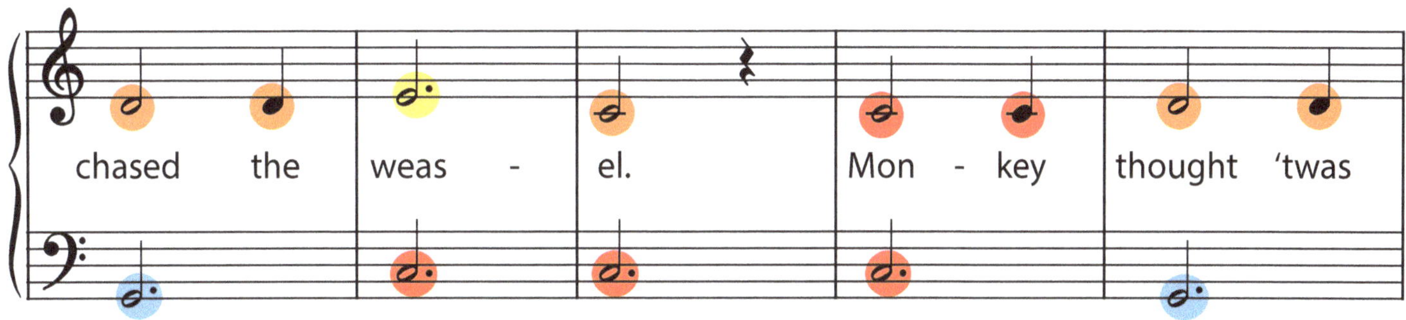

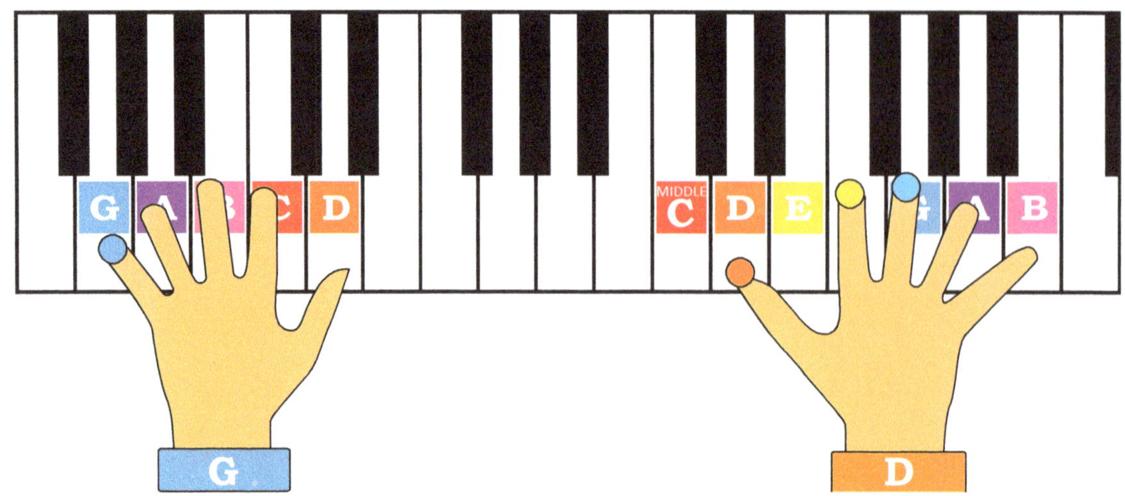

8. Old MacDonald

Keep the song going! Try out some more animals like our farm friends here and imitate their sounds!
moo moo here And a
moo moo there!
Here a moo! There a moo!
Eve-ry-where a moo moo!
Old Mac - Don - ald
had a farm,
E - I - E - I - O!

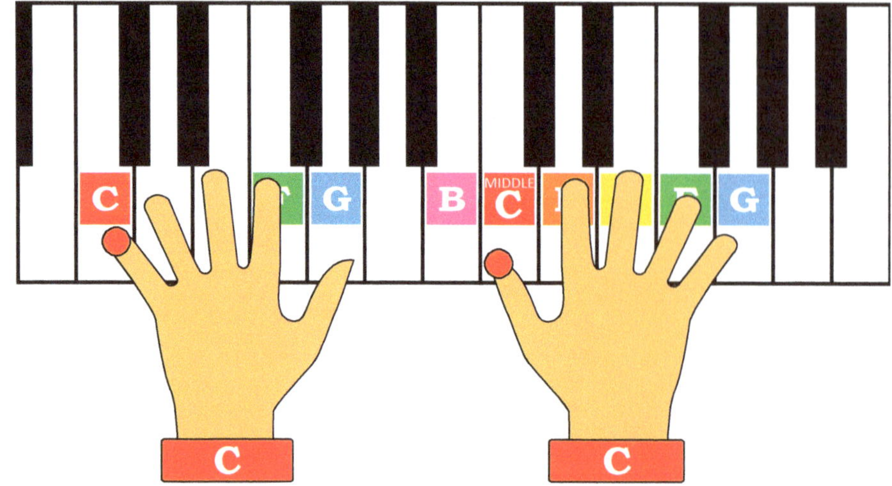

9. Polly Wolly Doodle

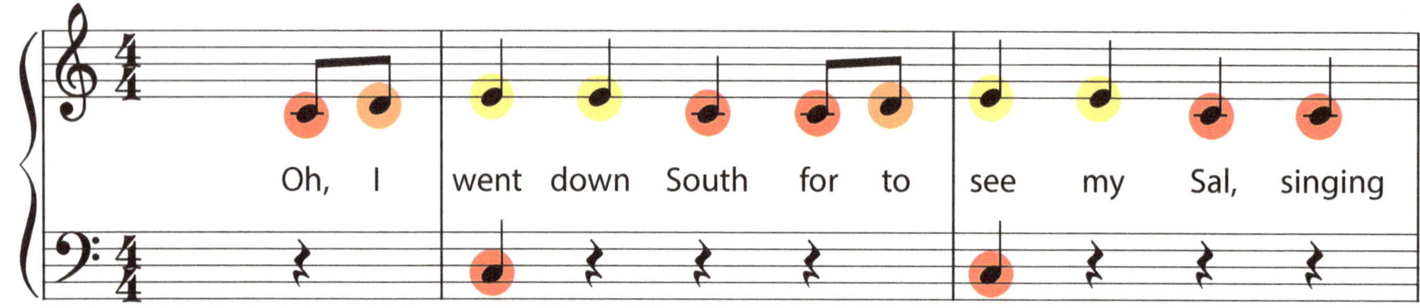

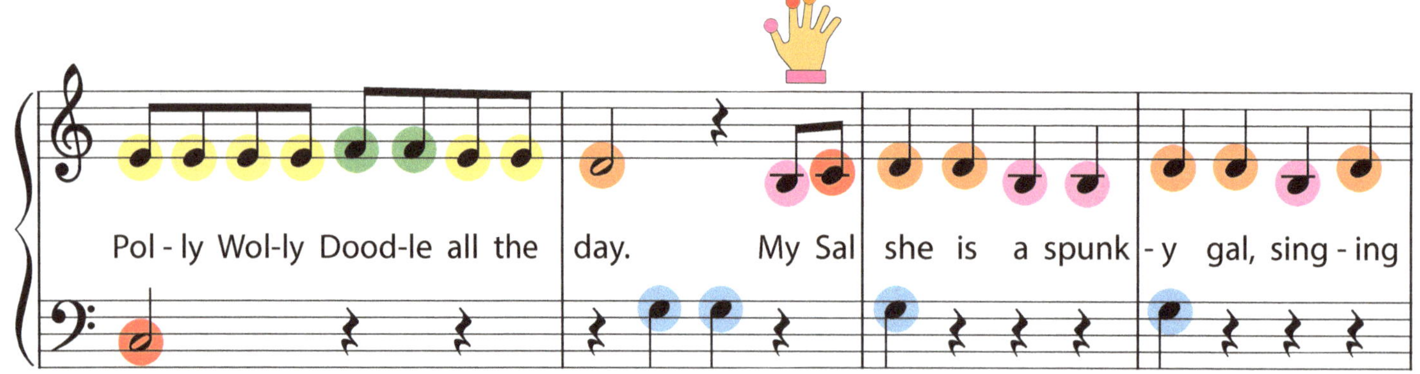

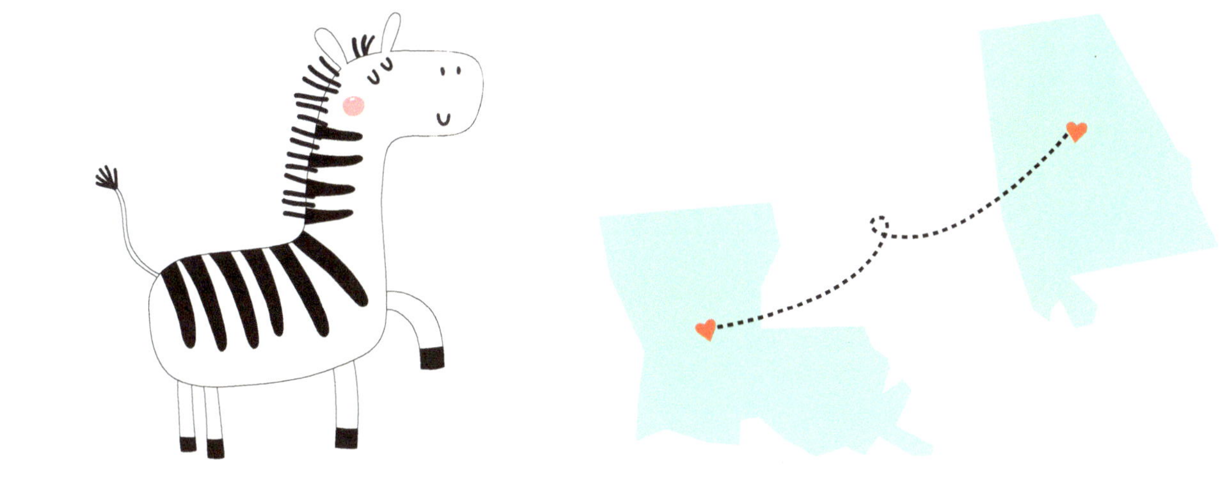

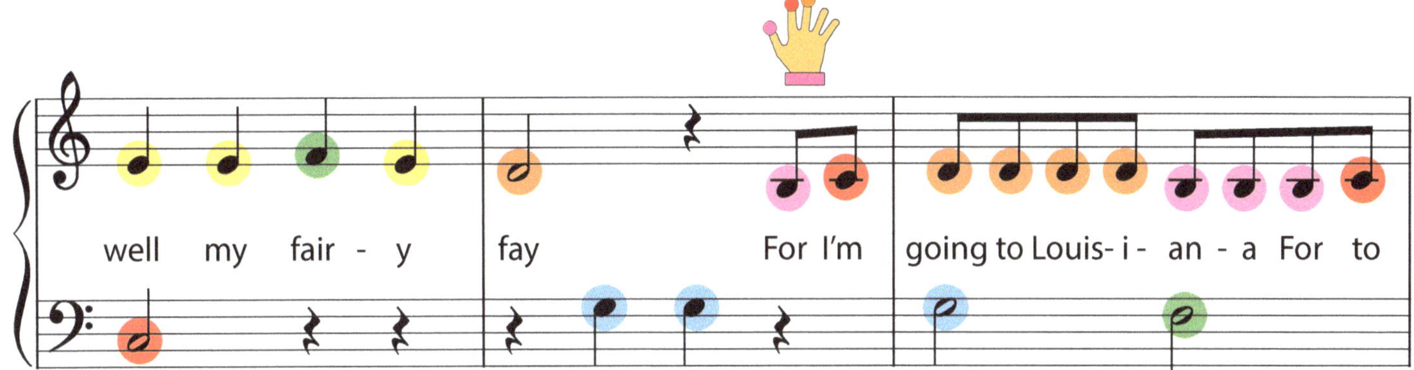
well my fair - y
fay For I'm
going to Louis- i - an - a For to

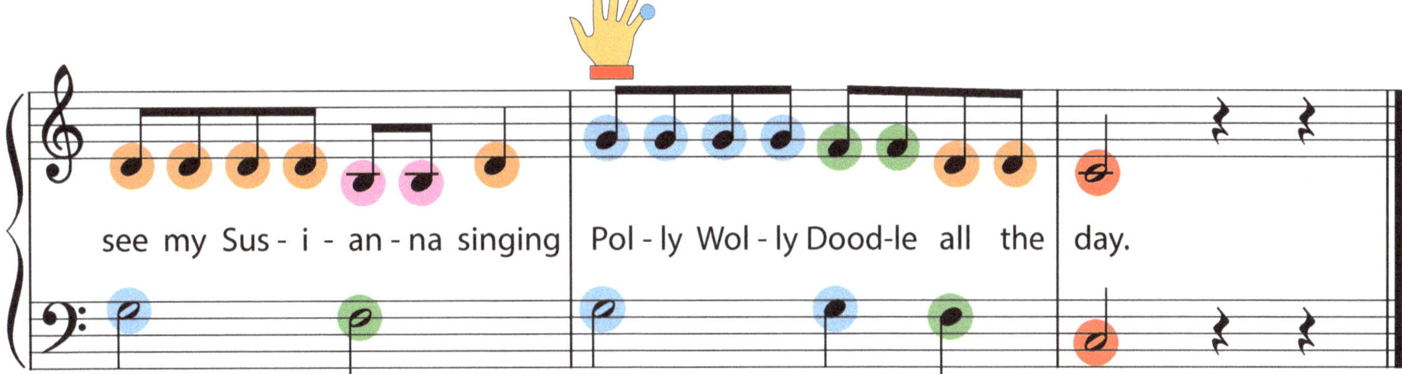
see my Sus - i - an - na singing
Pol - ly Wol - ly Dood-le all the
day.

10. If You're Happy and You Know It

If you're hap - py and you know it clap your hands! If you're
stomp your feet!

hap - py and you know it clap your hands! If you're hap-py and you know it and you
stomp your feet!

real - ly want to show it, if you're hap-py and you know it clap your hands!
stomp your feet!

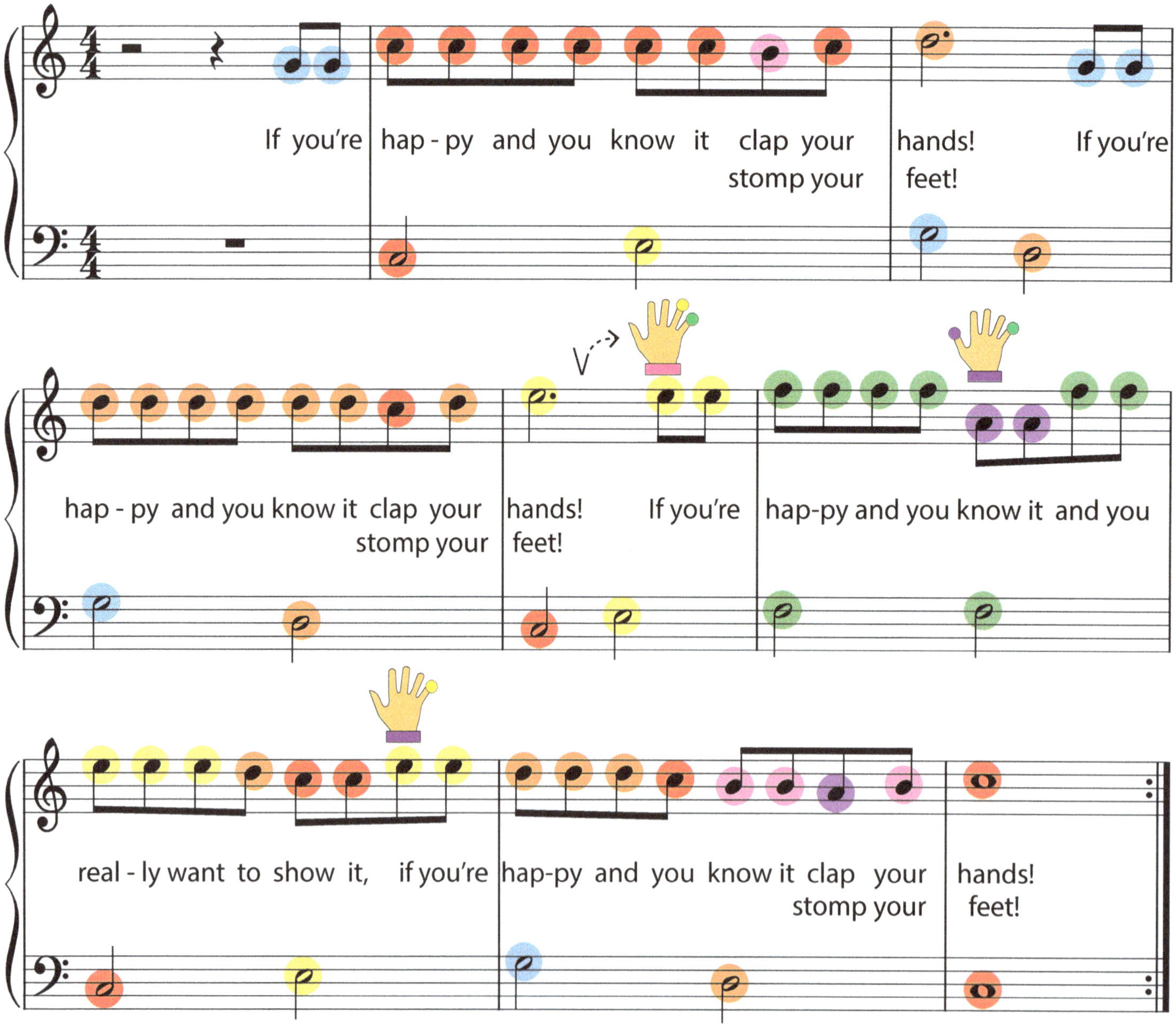

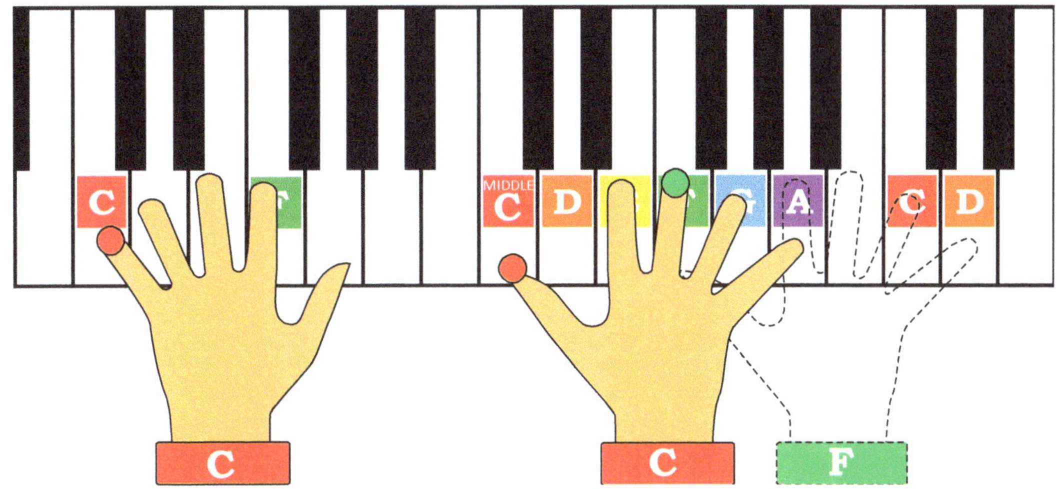

11. A-Hunting We Will Go

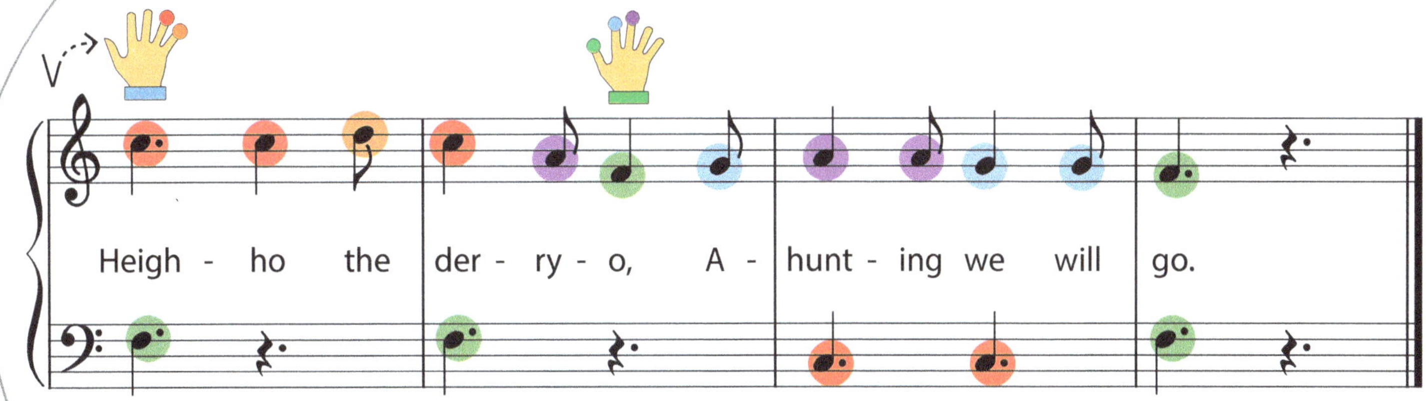

New!

When there are 6 beats per measure, an eighth note ♪ gets 1 beat

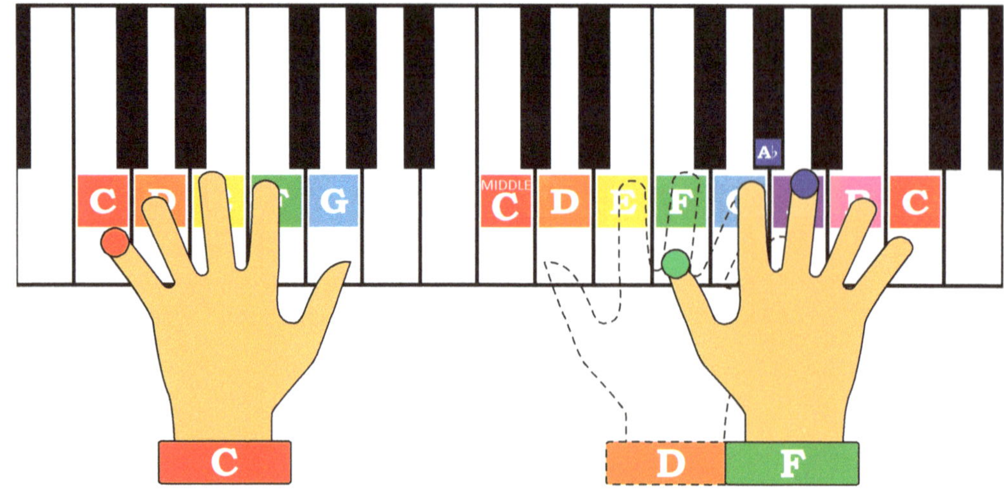
C
D
E
F
G
MIDDLE C
D
E
F
G
A♭
B
C
C
D
F

12. O Sole Mio

12

Ma n'a-tu so - le, Cchiù bel - lo, oi ne', 'o so - le mi - o,

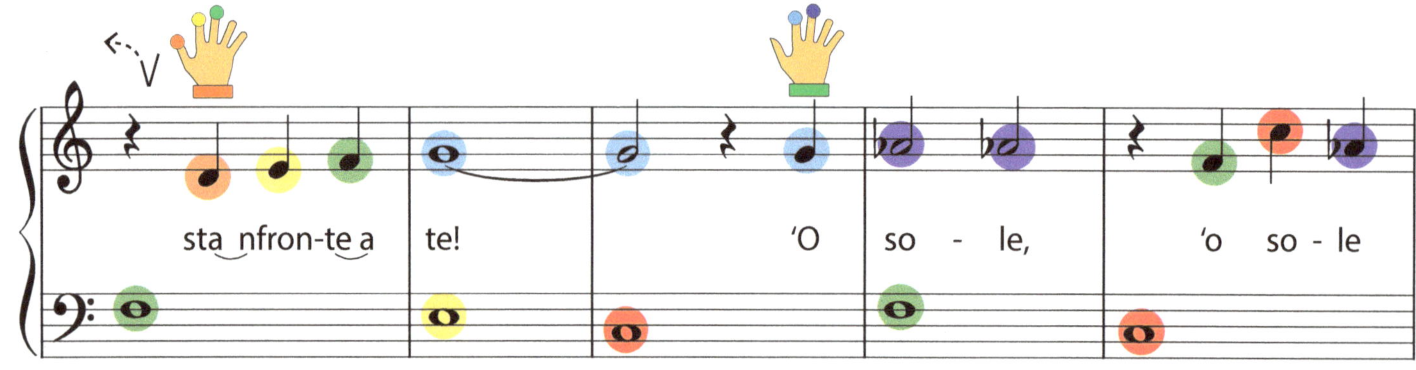
sta nfron-te a te! 'O so - le, 'o so - le

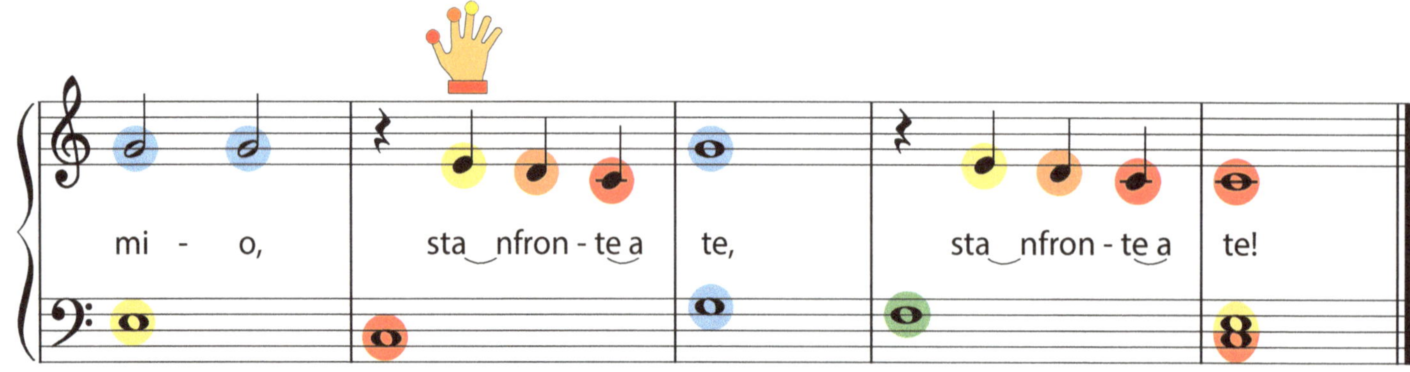
mi - o, sta nfron - te a te, sta nfron - te a te!

13. Five Little Monkeys

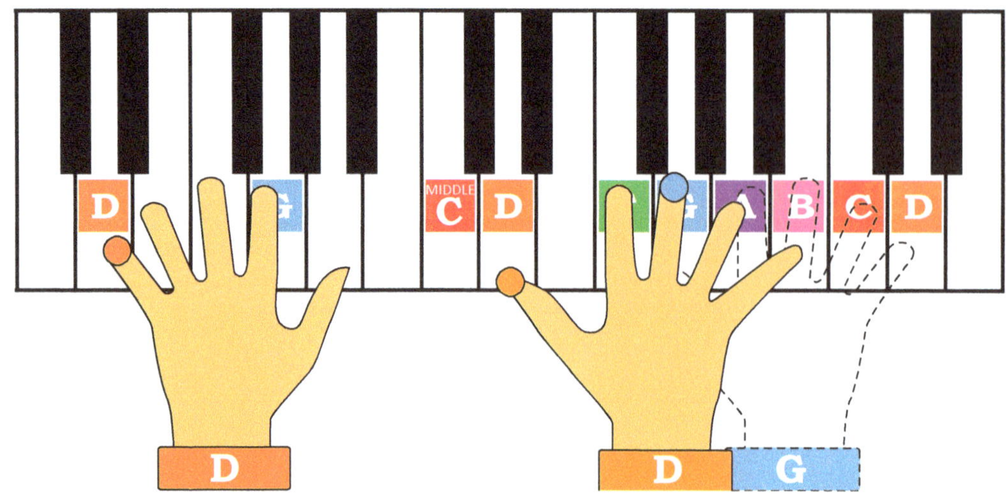

14. Alouette

New! 8

Jump a full octave in the arrow's direction.

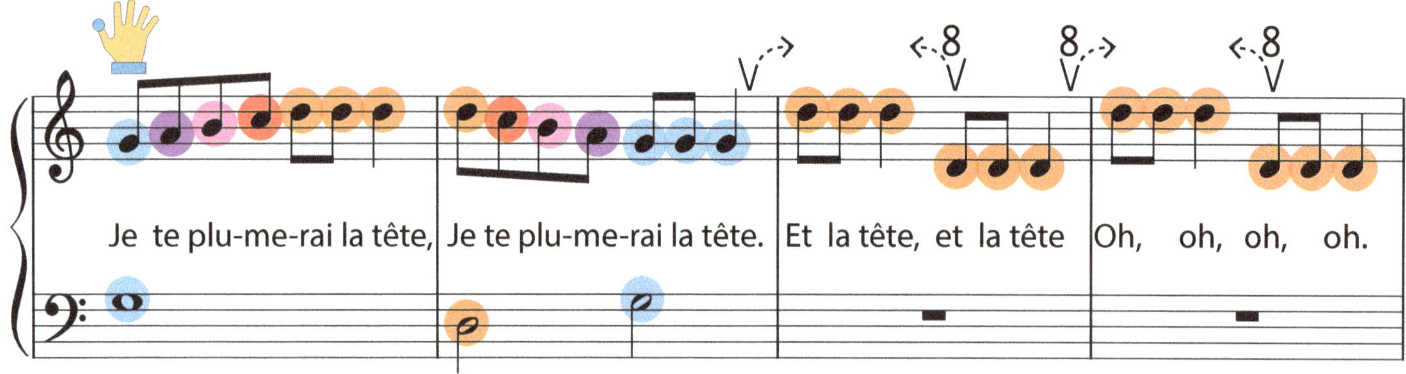

Exercise 3: The 7-Key Arpeggio

Now let's try stretching the hands even further! We'll go from the 6-key stretch to a 7-key stretch in this exercise.

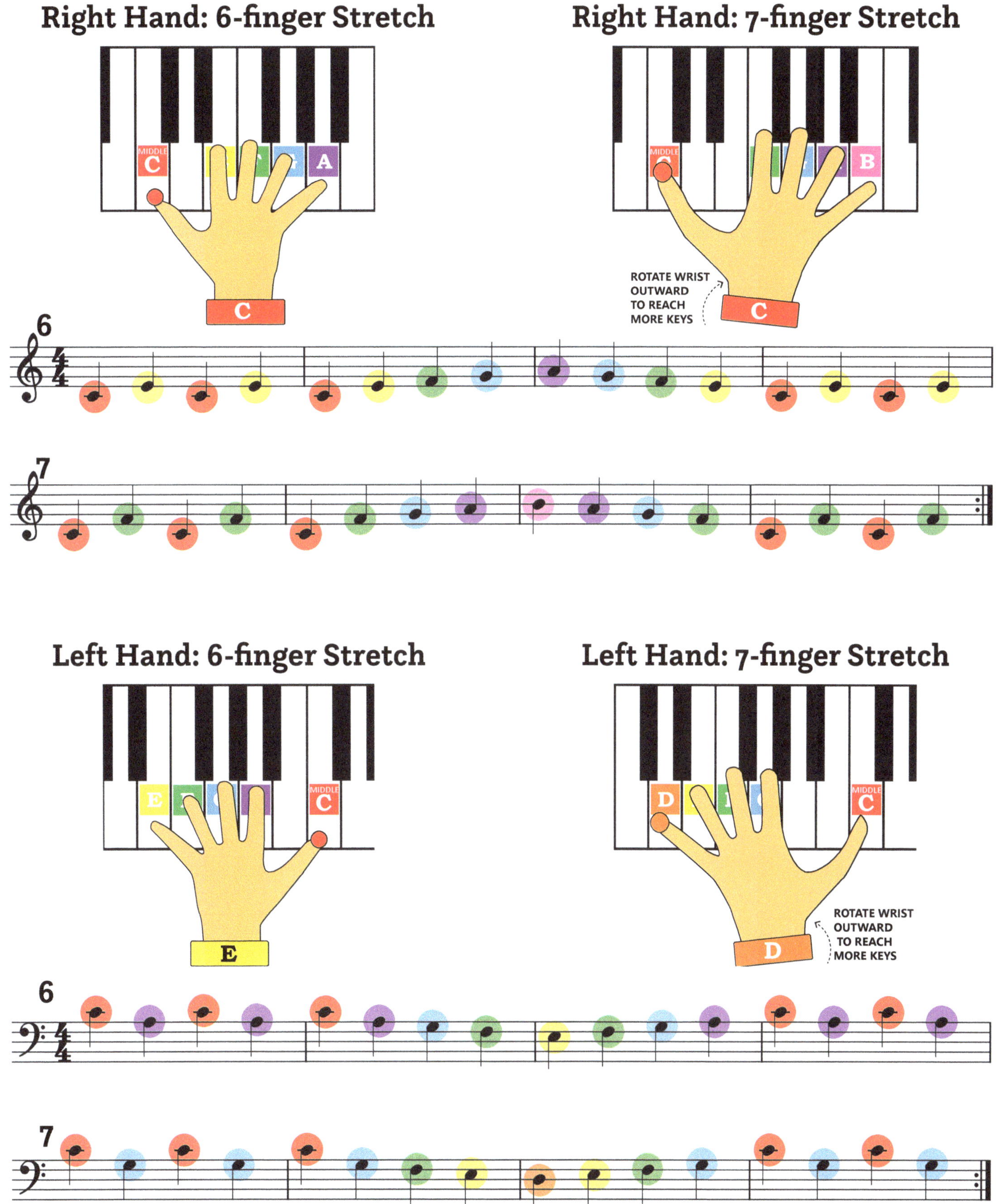

Exercise 4: The 8-Key Arpeggio

For the next song, we'll stretch even further! Finger 5 will skip a key to play notes across a full octave C to C. Stay loose and relaxed, and be ready to **rotate** and move your wrist and forearm to help your fingers reach the wider intervals.

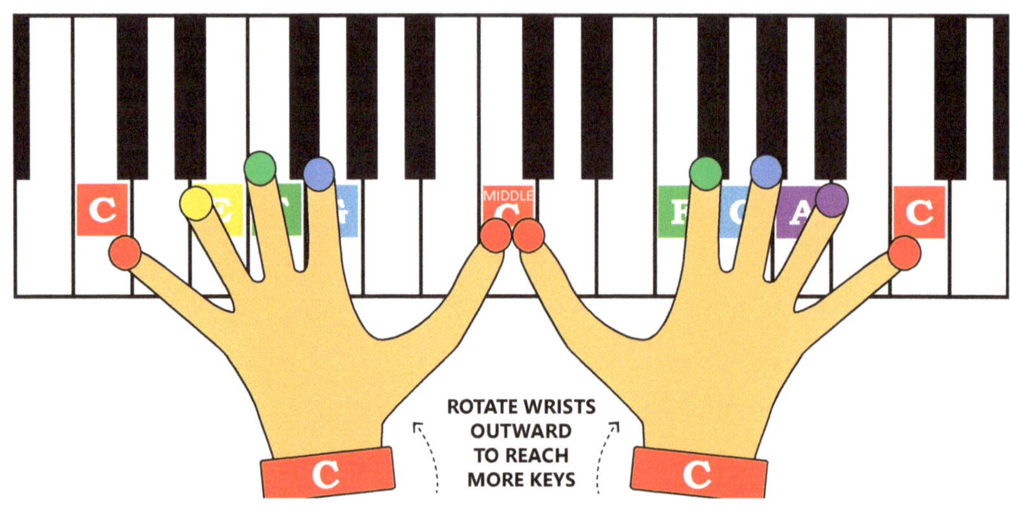

Right Hand — Repeat 3x

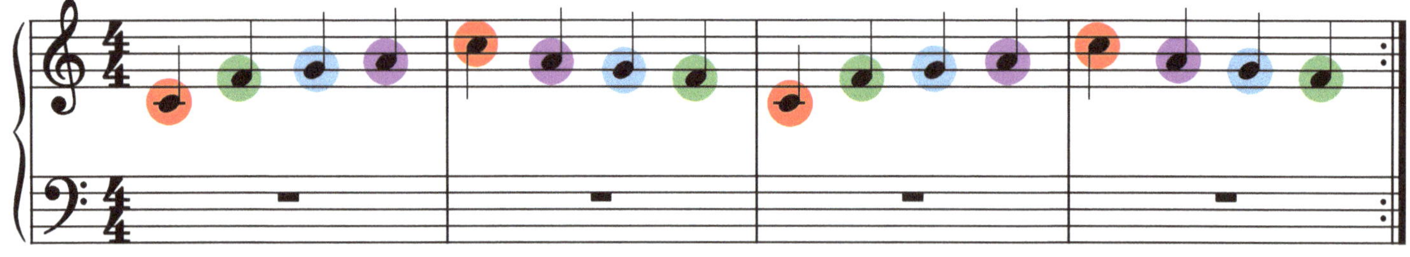

Left Hand — Repeat 3x

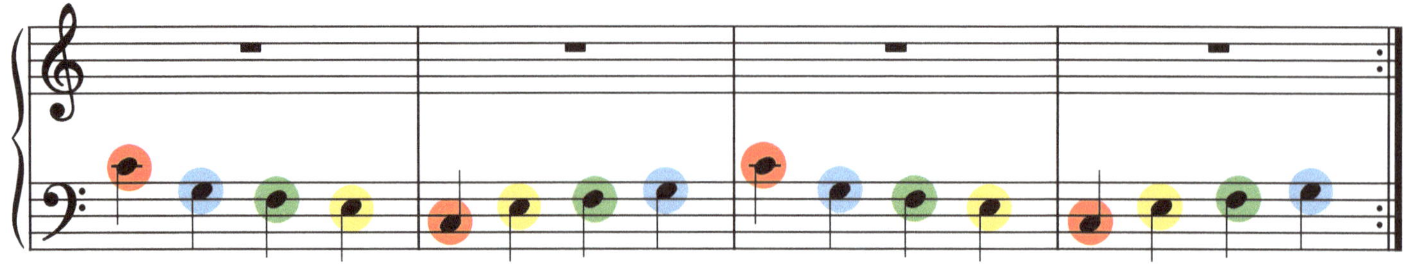

15. The Wheels on the Bus

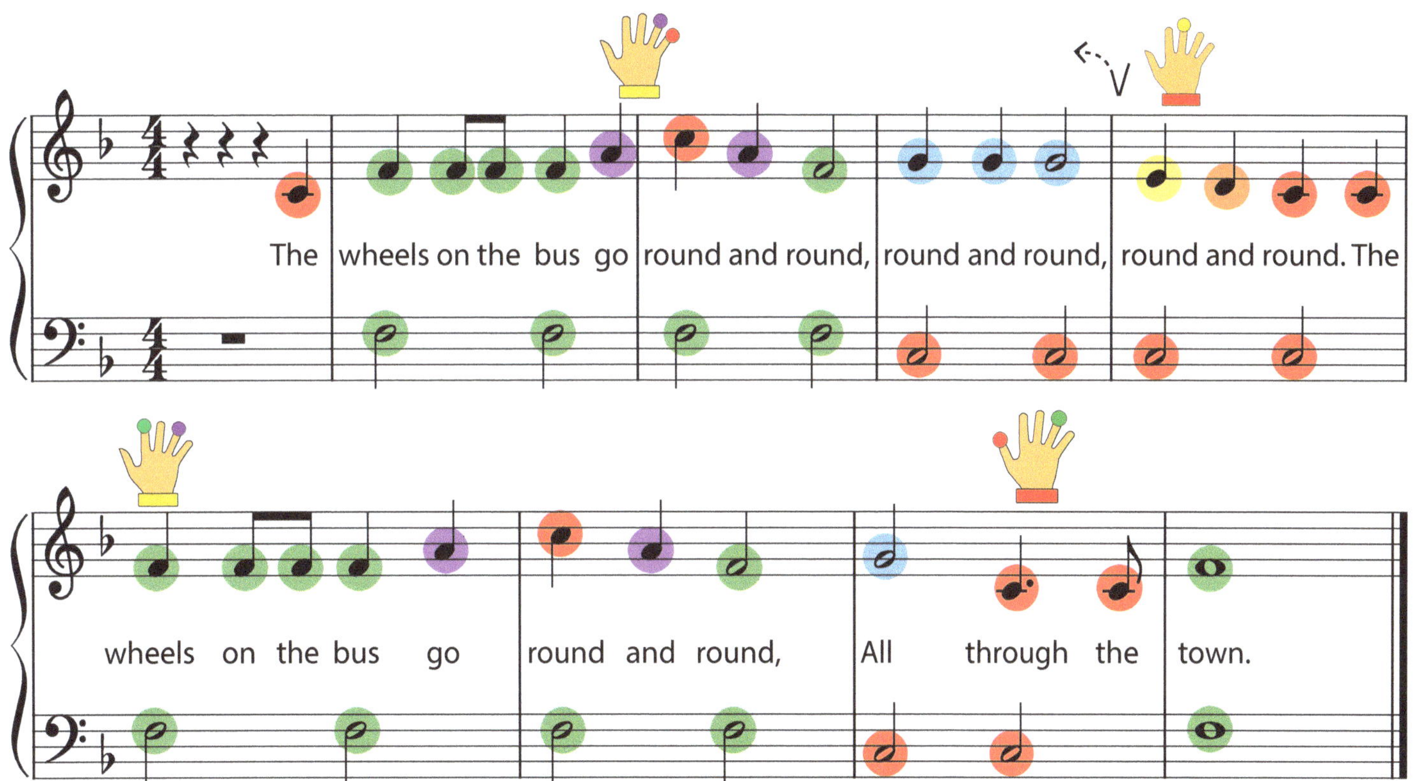

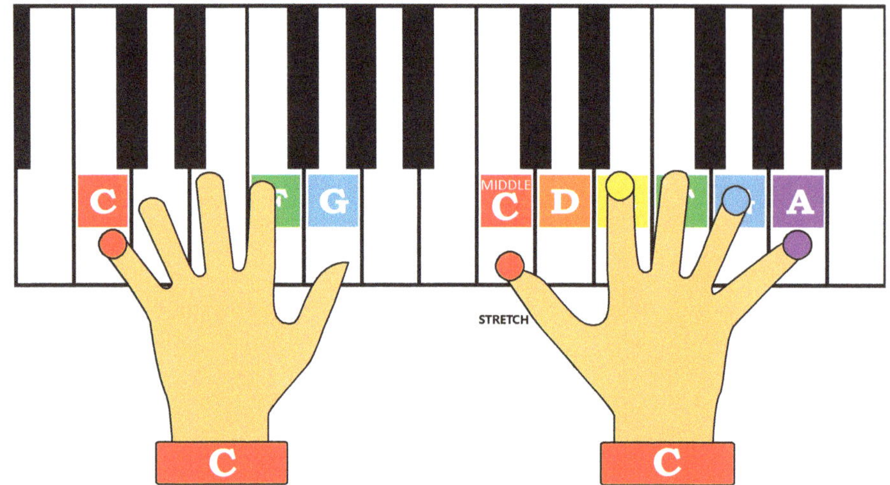

16. Kum Ba Yah

16

New!

Hold the note through the tie.

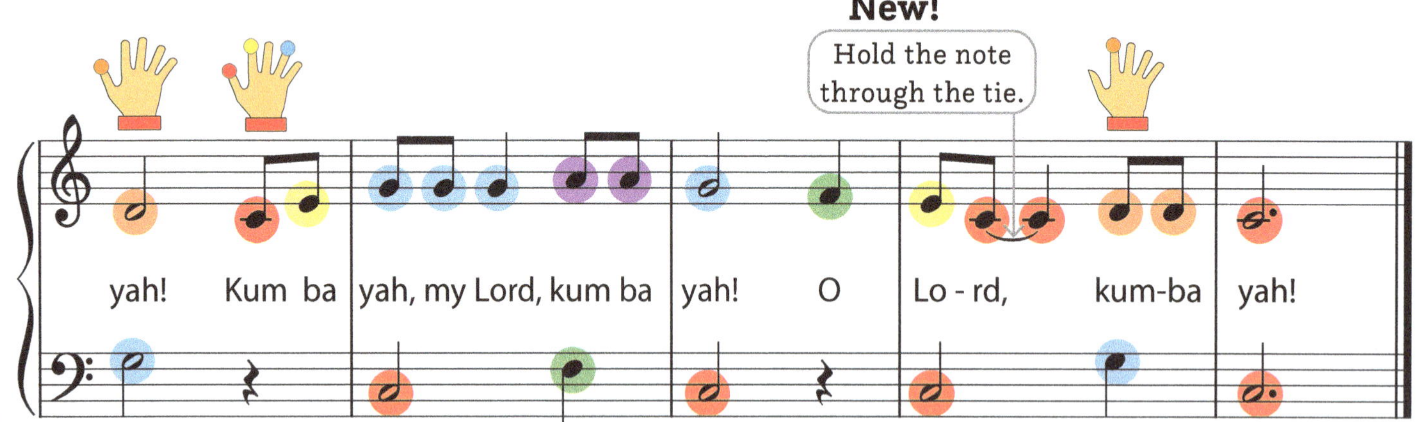

Exercise 5: Finger Crossing

Sometimes a series of notes require your fingers to walk up or down the keyboard.

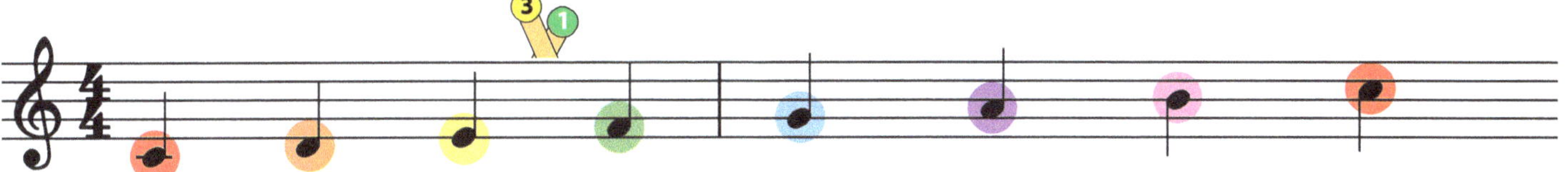

In this example, walking up the keyboard with your right hand requires you to **thumb under** finger 3.

If you return down the keyboard from high C, **cross over** the thumb with finger 3.

Arch fingers 2 & 3, to allow the thumb to go beneath, as shown:

The thumb reaches F by going under the arched fingers 2 and 3.

After the cross-over, the fingers return to their natural position to play the next notes.

Let's try some exercises on the next page!

Exercise 5a: Finger Crossing: 1 & 2

ONLY USE FINGERS 1 & 2 to walk your fingers up and down the keyboard in the exercises below. The finger diagrams will help guide your fingers.

Right Hand — Thumb Under

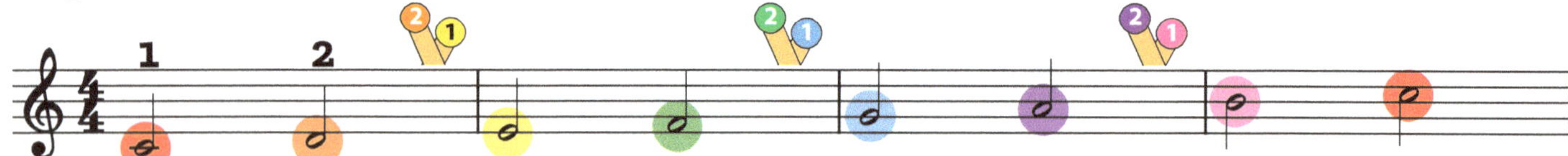

Right Hand — Finger Over

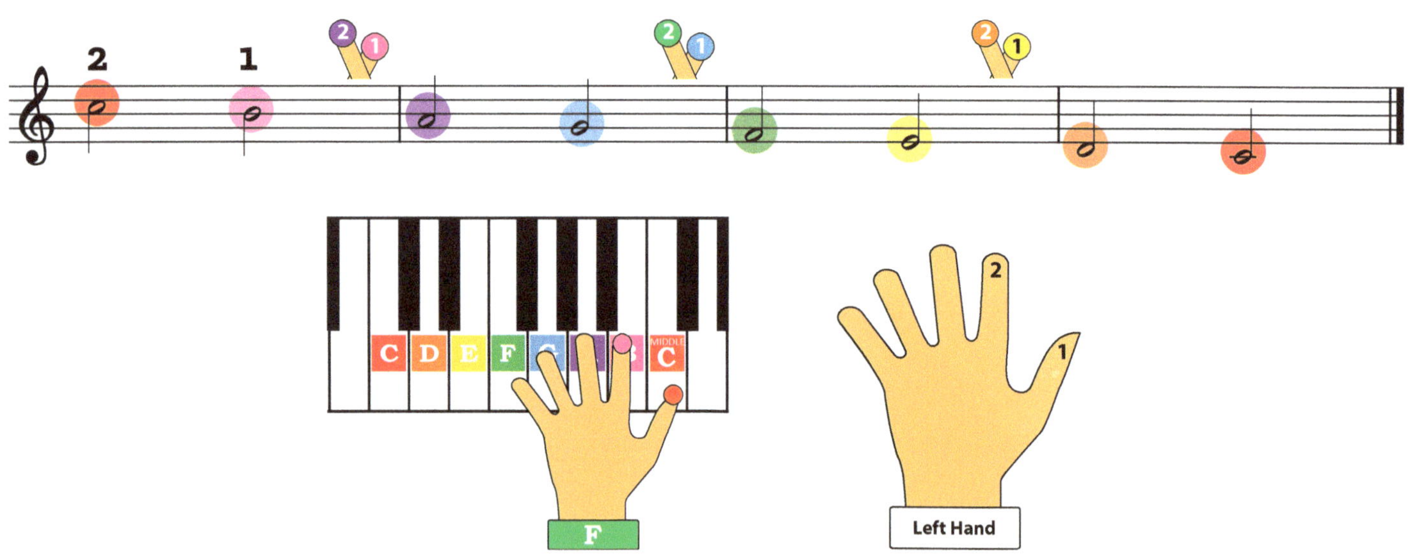

Left Hand — Thumb Under

Left Hand — Finger Over

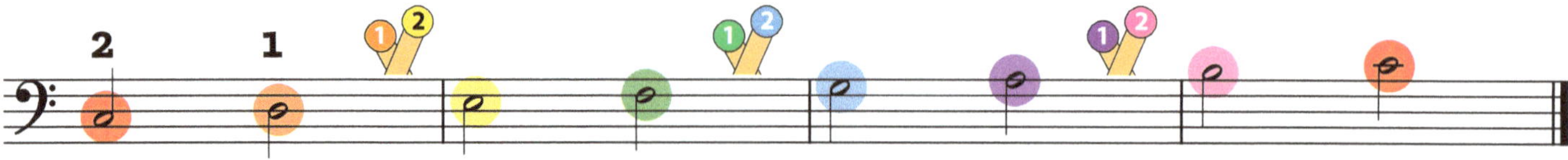

Exercise 5b: Finger Crossing: 1 & 3

ONLY USE FINGERS 1, 2, & 3 to play the exercises below.

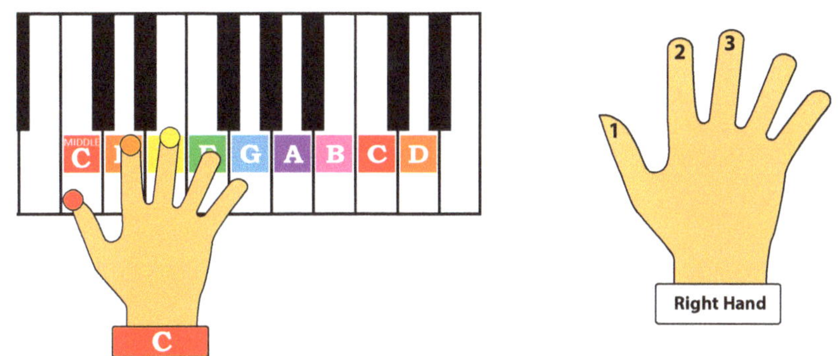

Right Hand — Thumb Under

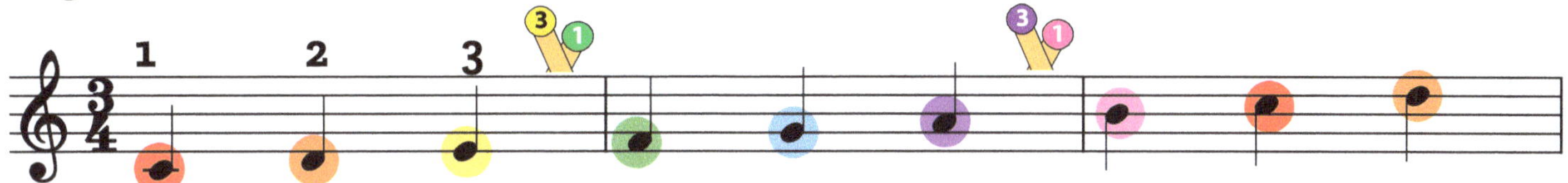

Right Hand — Finger Over

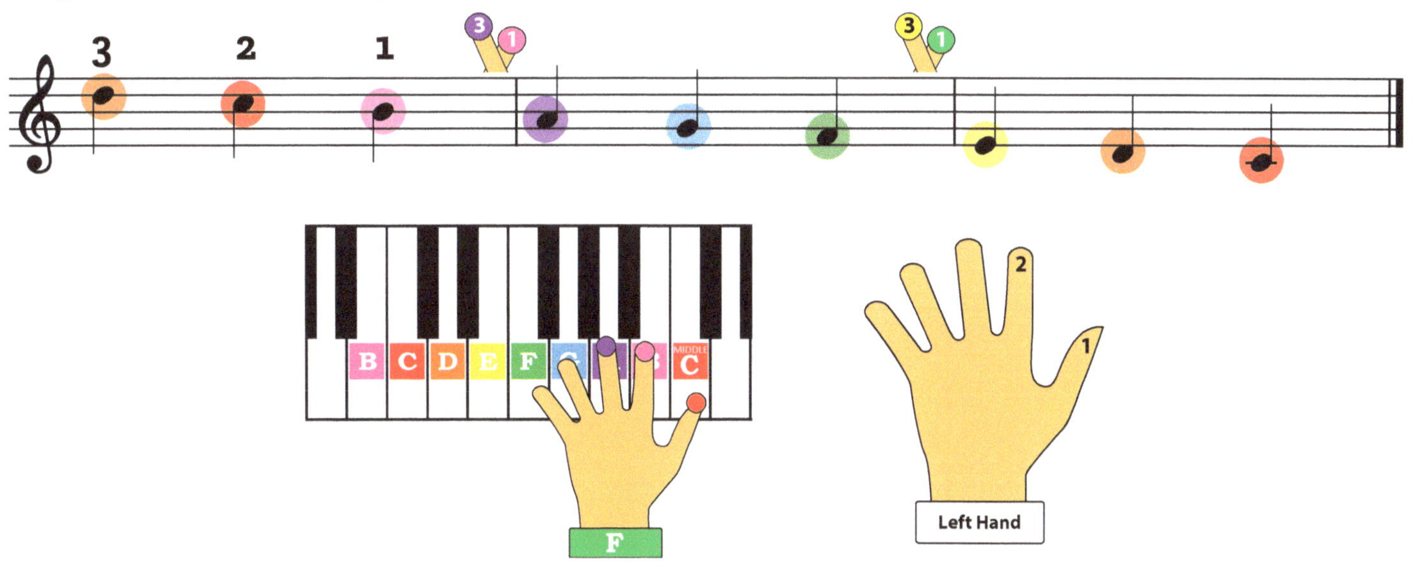

Left Hand — Thumb Under

Left Hand — Finger Over

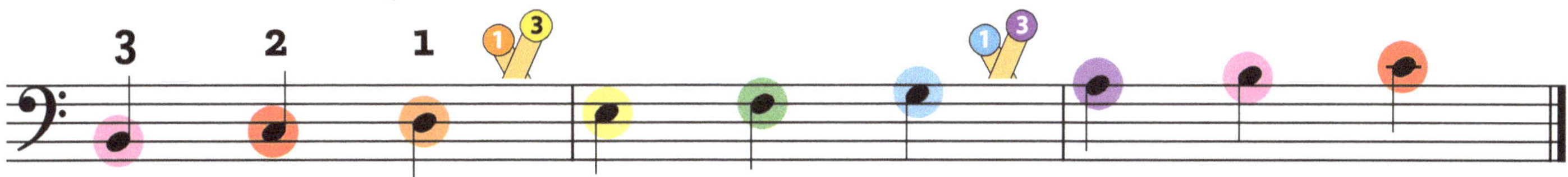

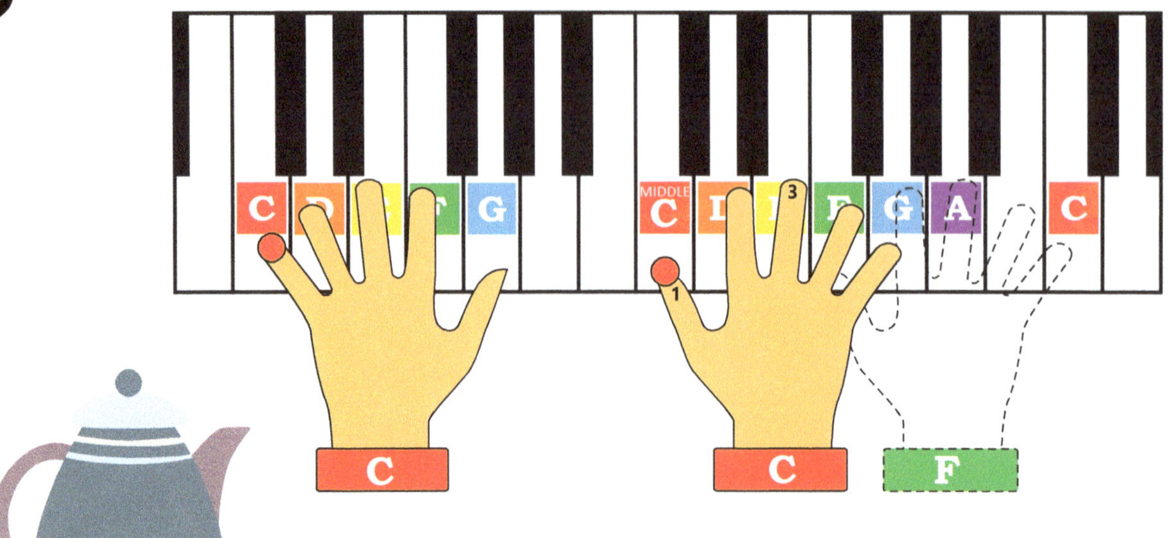

17. I'm A Little Teapot

17

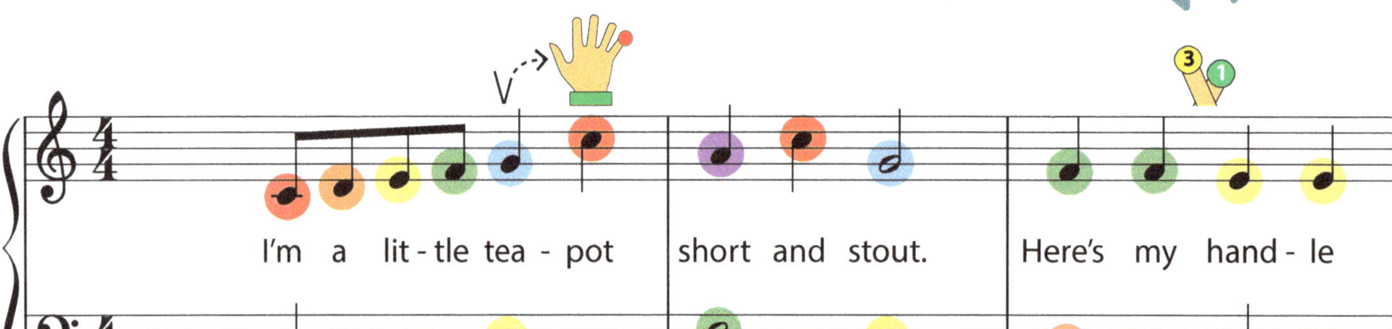

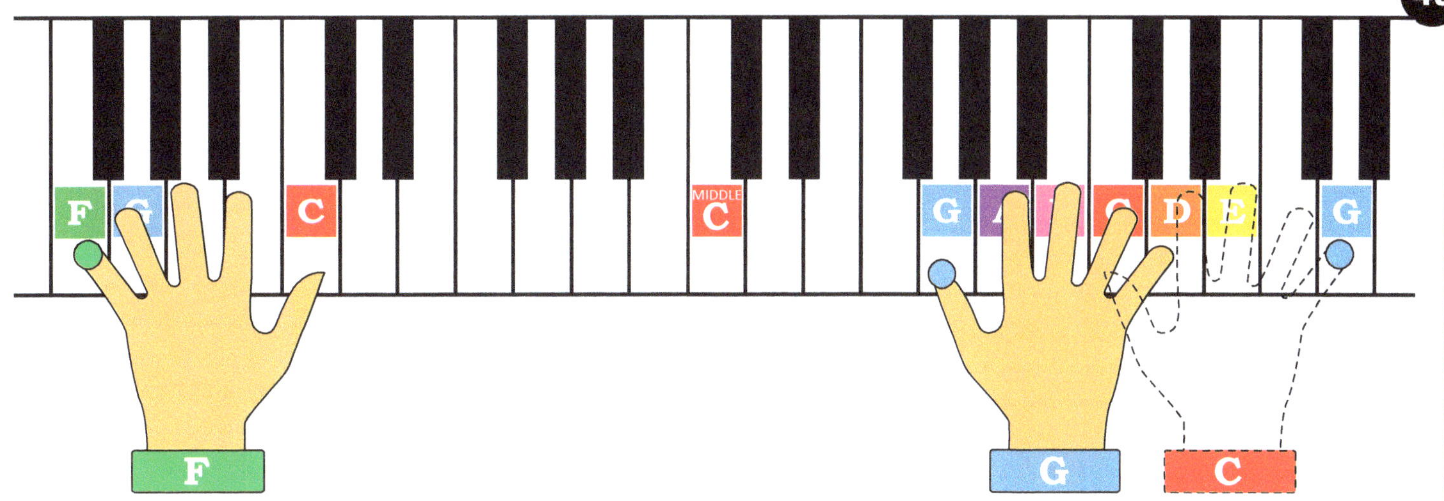

18. Happy Birthday

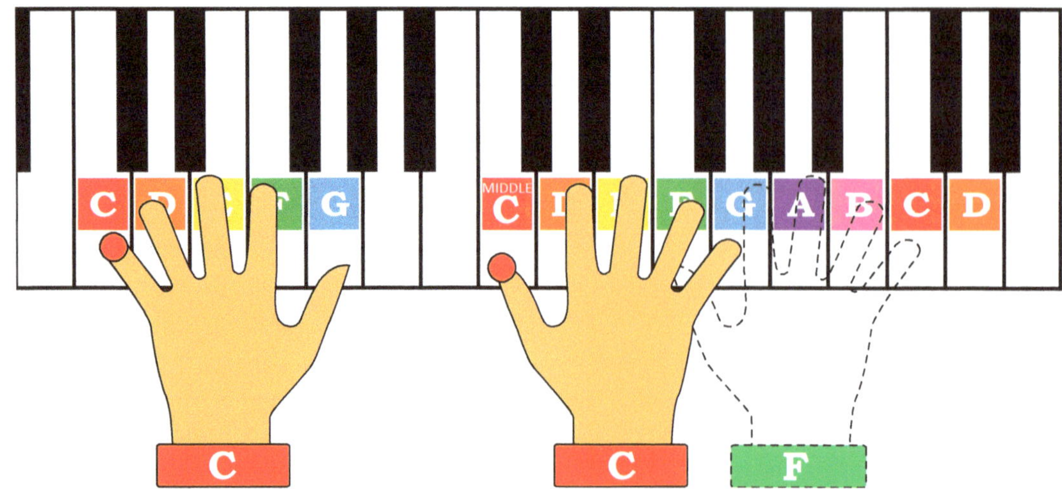

19. Three Blind Mice

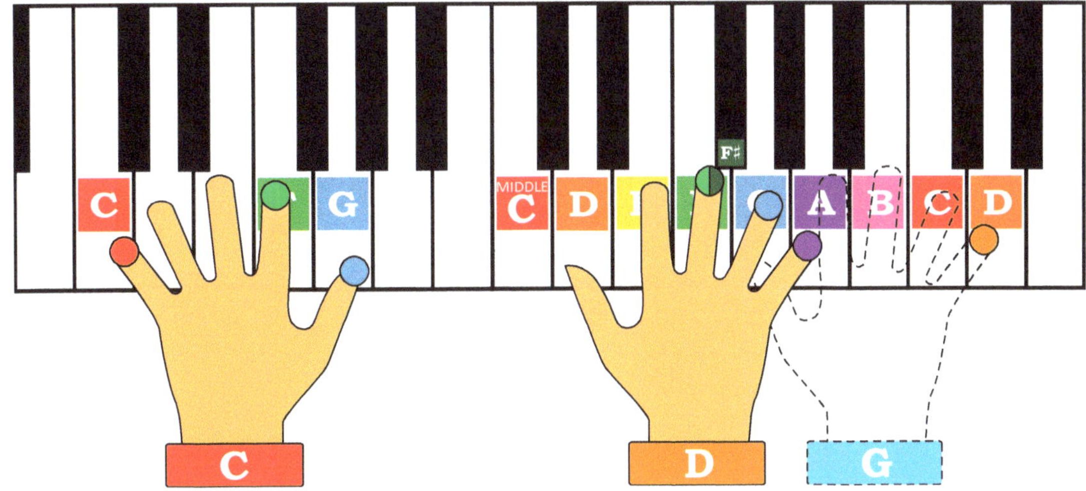

20. Head, Shoulders, Knees, and Toes

Head, shoul - ders, knees, and toes, knees and toes. Head, shoul - ders, knees, and

toes, knees and to - es. A - nd eyes and ears and

mo - uth a - nd nose. Head, shoul - ders, knees, and toes, knees and toes.

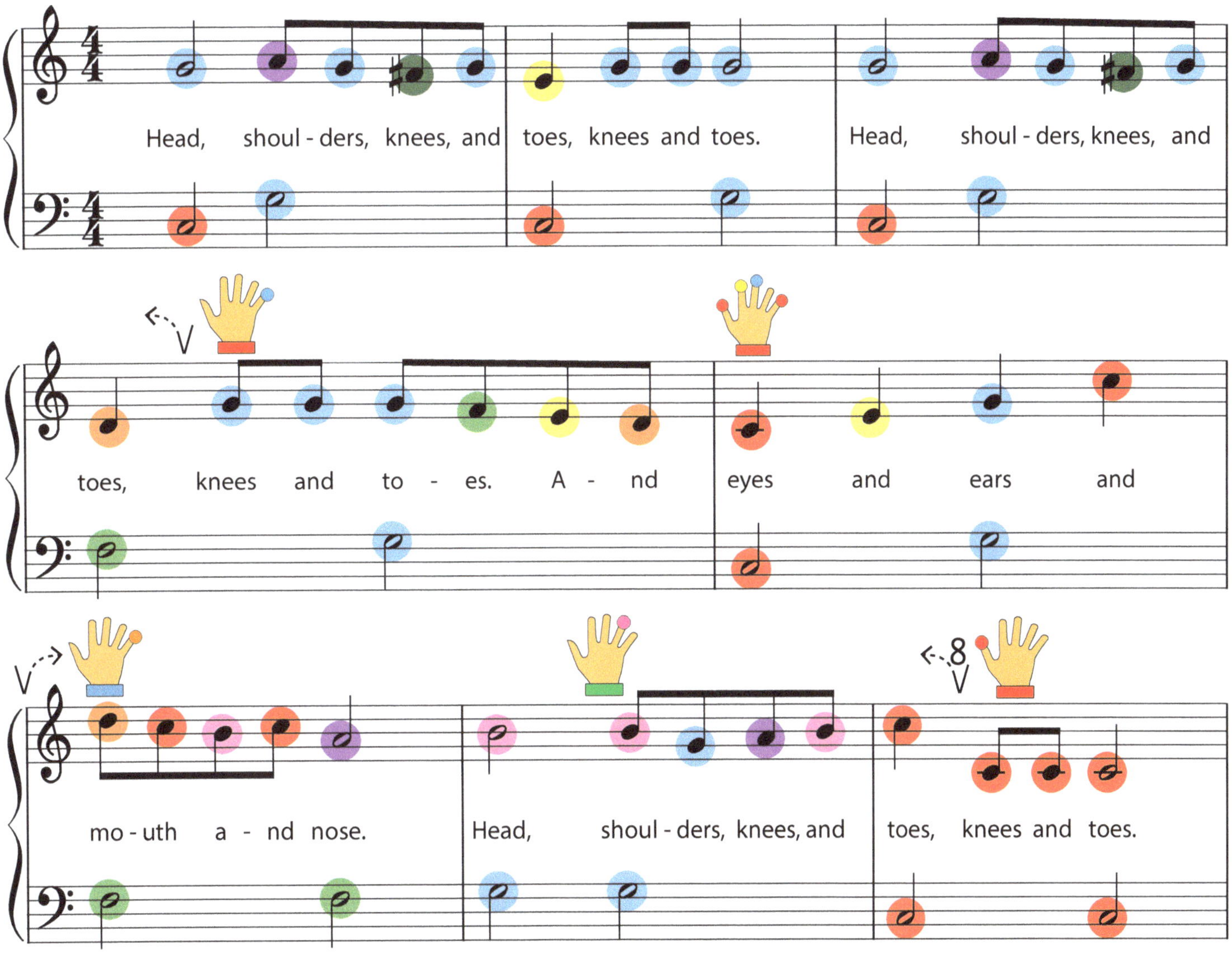

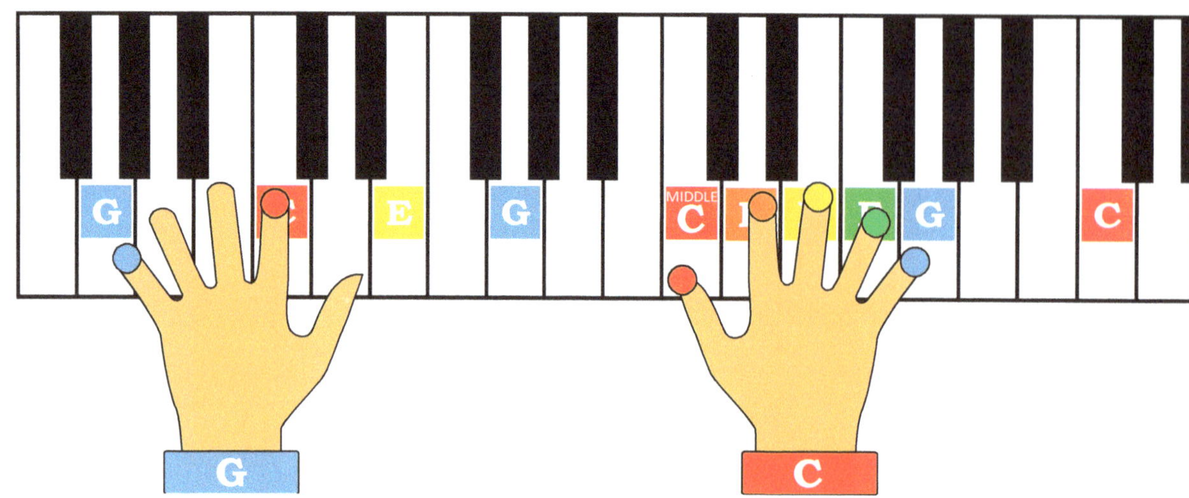

21. Row, Row, Row Your Boat

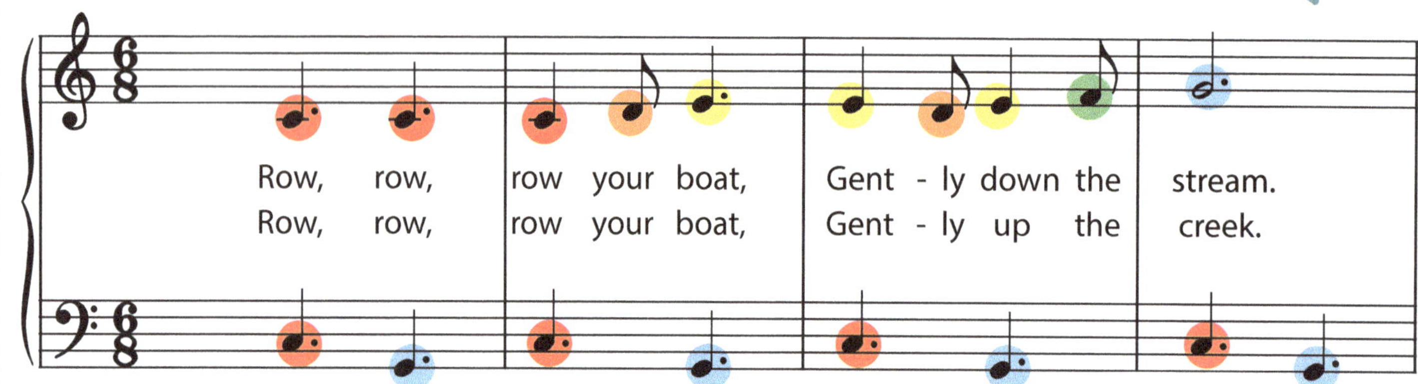

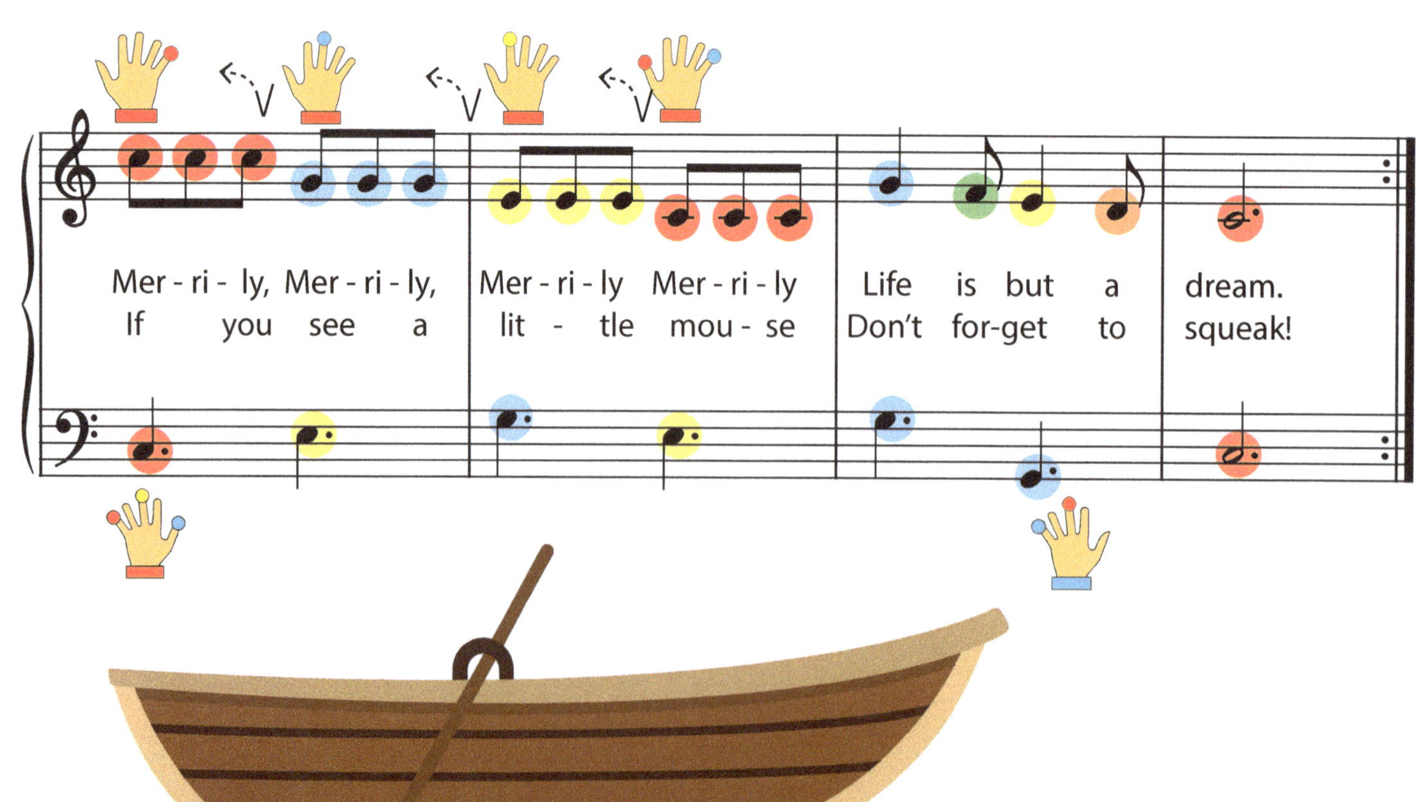

Exercise 6: Playing Octaves

Now that you can play the 8-key Arpeggio, let's practice playing Octaves—2 notes with the same name, 8 keys apart. You will only use fingers 1 and 5 to play the notes.

1. Elevate the wrist slightly so you don't accidentaly play the black keys with fingers 2, 3, and 4.
2. Turn the hand at the wrist to widen finger reach.
3. Use a light touch with both finger and thumb. Make a little jump as needed.

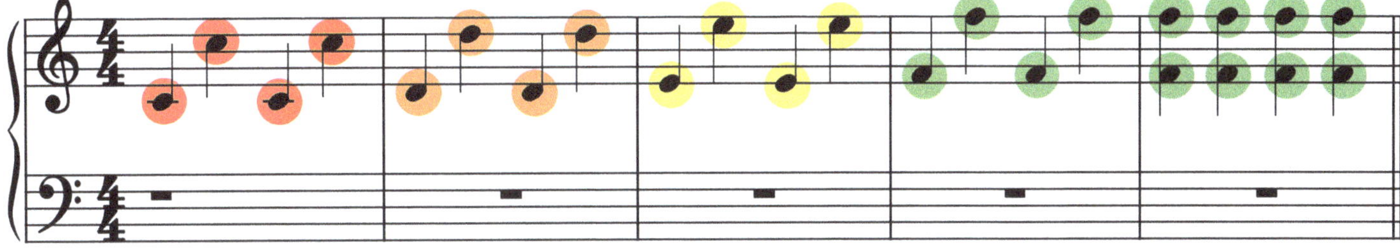

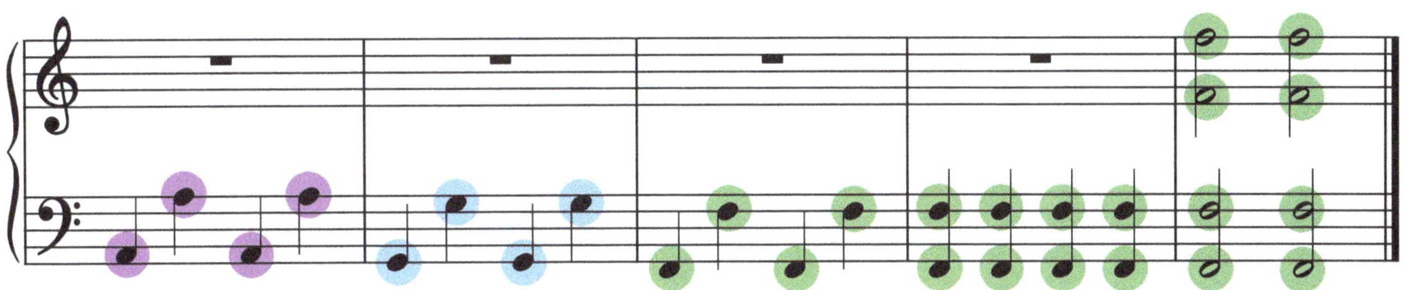

This symbol: 8 means you will jump an octave!

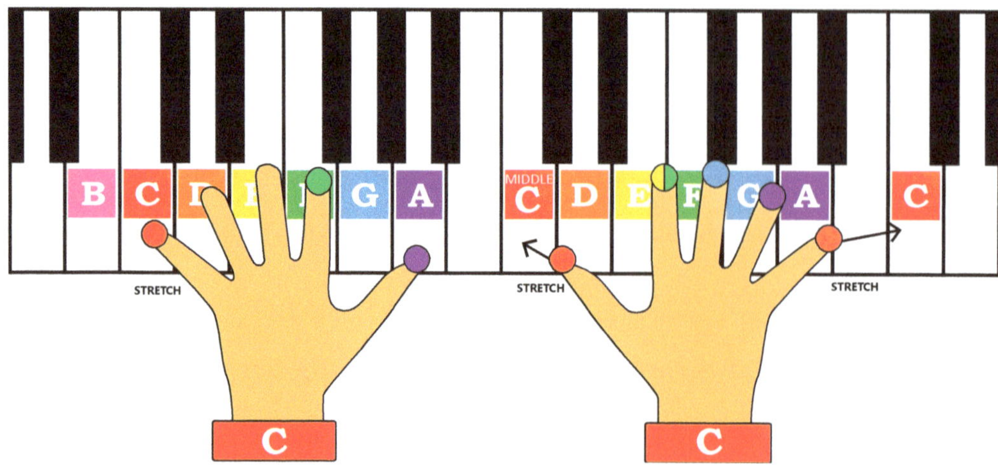

22. On Top of Spaghetti

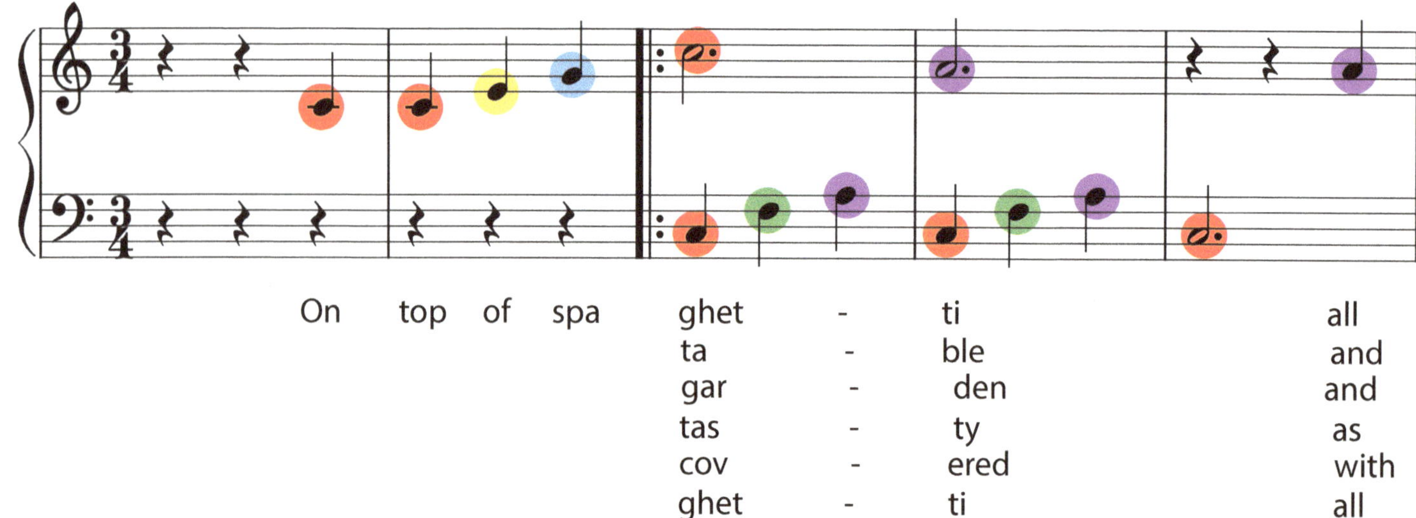

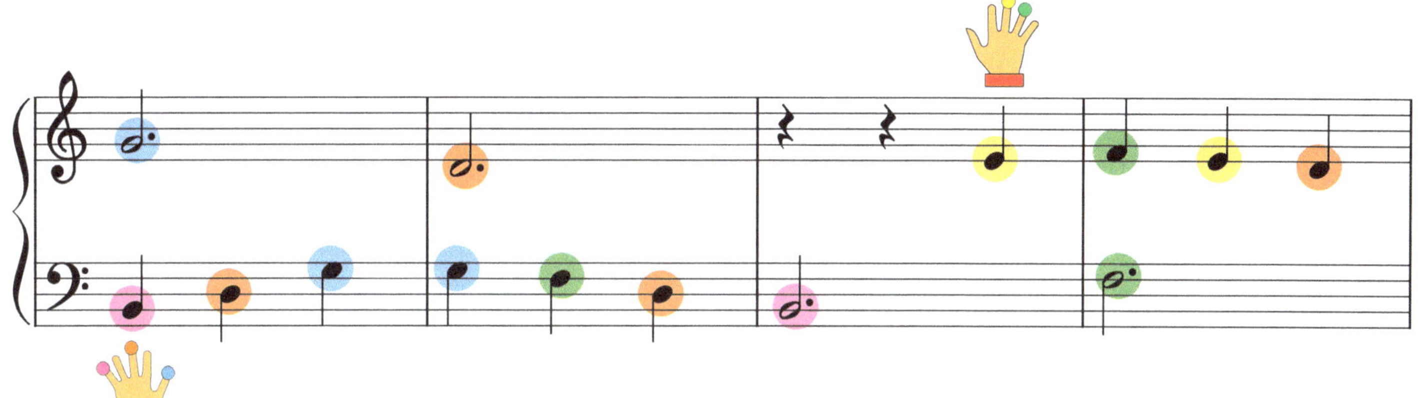

meat - ball when some - bod - y
meat - ball rolled right out the
meat - ball was noth - ing but
sum - mer grew in - to a
meat - balls and to - ma - to
meat - balls and don't e - ver

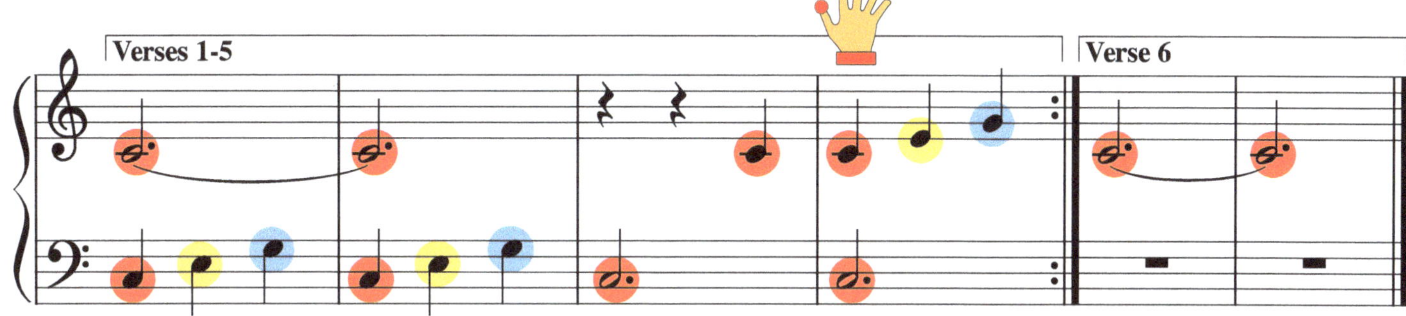

sneezed.__________ It rolled off the
door.__________ It rolled through the
mush.__________ The mush was as
tree.__________ The tree was all
sauce.__________ If you eat spa-

sneeze!

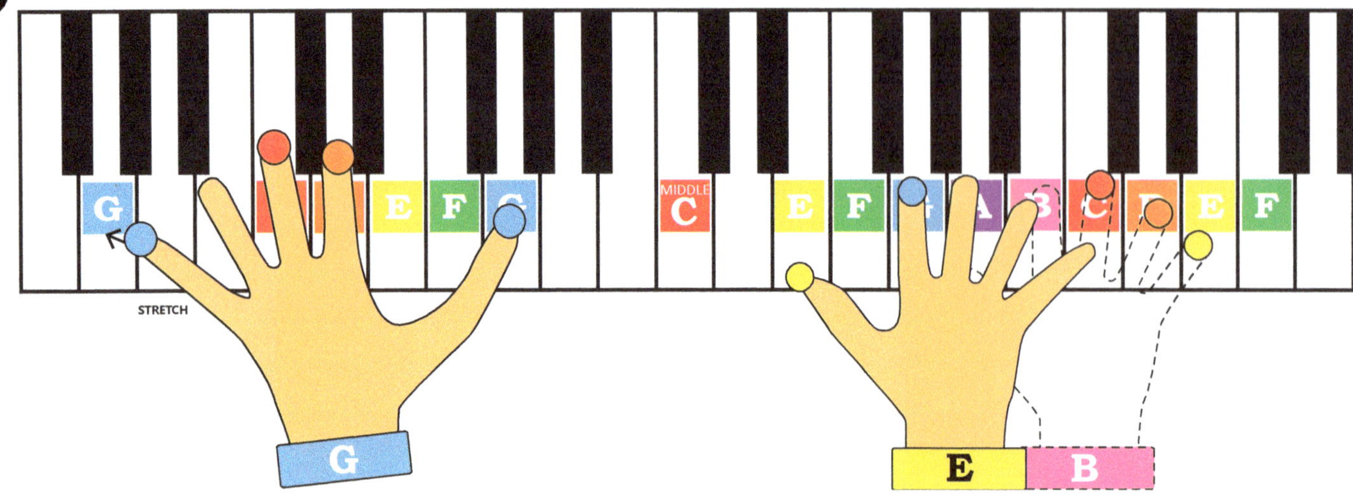

23. Rock-a-Bye Baby

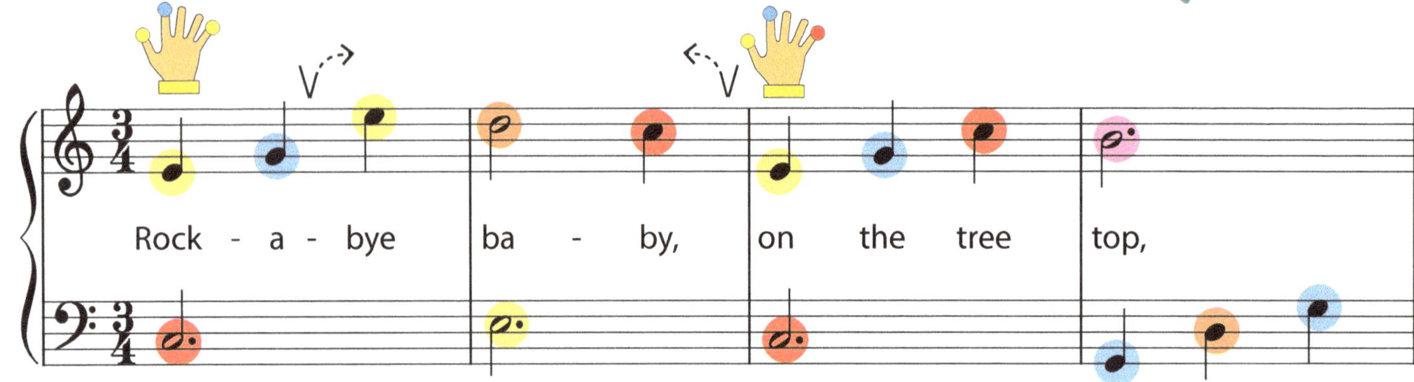

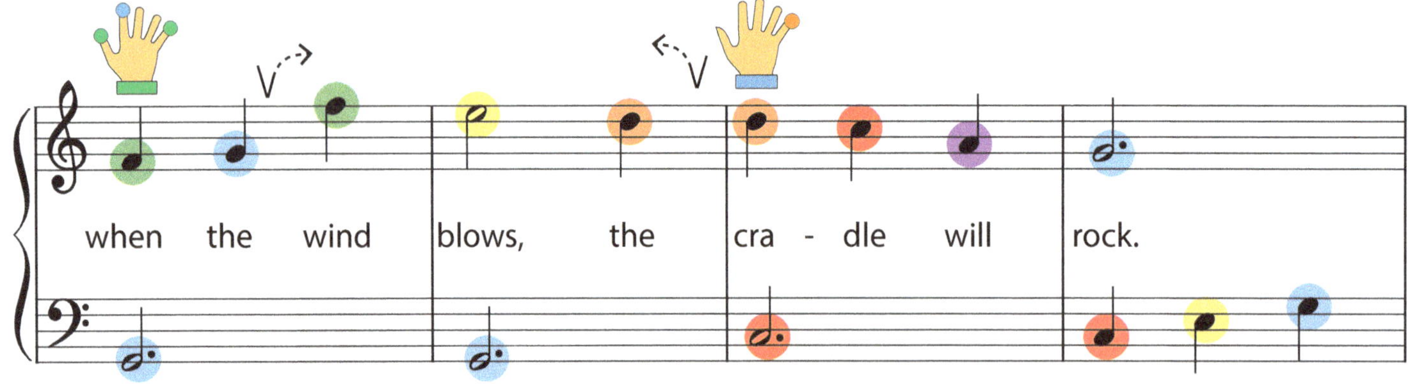

When the bough breaks, the cra - dle will fall, and
down will come ba - by, cra - dle and all!

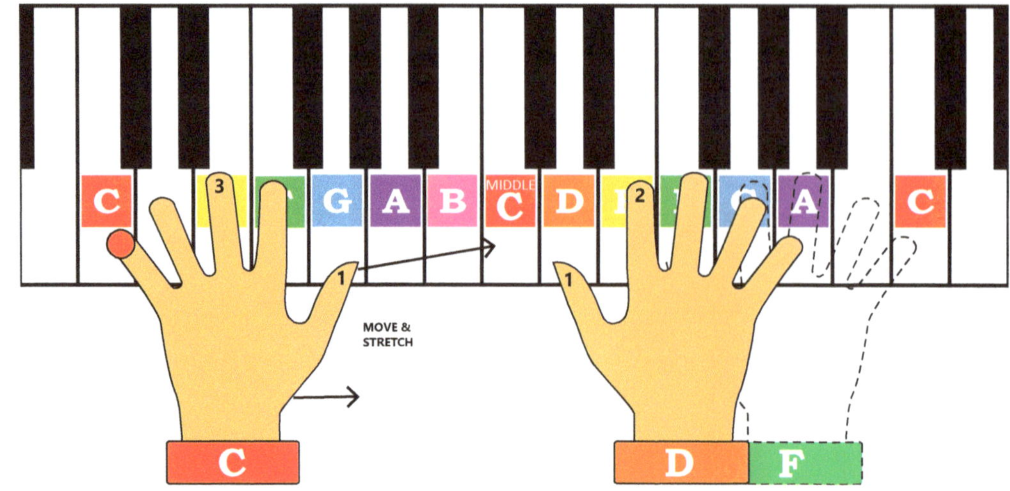

24. Camptown Races

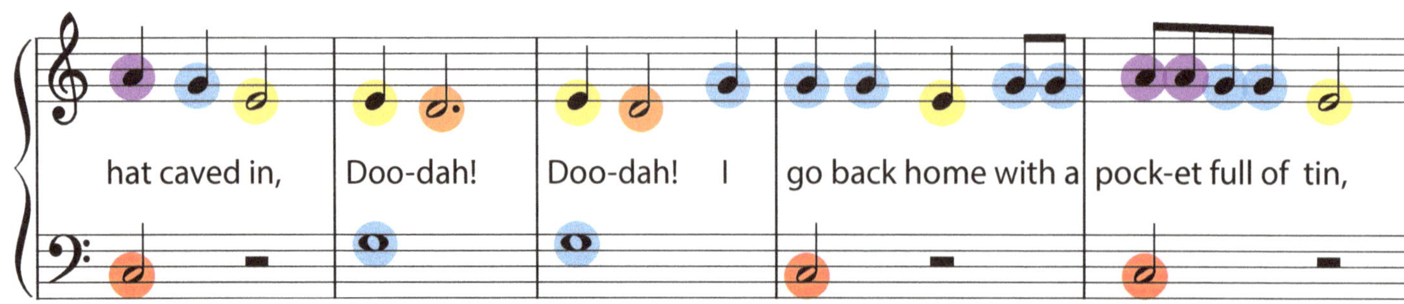

2
1
Oh, doo-dah day! Goin' to run all night, Goin' to run all
2
1
day; I'll bet my money on the bob-tail nag, Some-bod-y bet on the bay.
1
3

Top Tips for Keeping Time

Practice your music in phrases, or chunks, of two or three measures at a time. Repeat this to get used to the motion required for that sequence.

Learn just the notes first, then make sure you're playing each note for the right amount of time. This is called the rhythm. A helpful tool to help you keep time is a **metronome**.

A metronome is a special tool that helps you keep a steady beat when you play music. It makes a clicking sound—tick, tick, tick—like a clock. Each tick is one beat. You can set it to go fast or slow, depending on the song you're learning. When you play along with the clicks, it helps you stay in time and not speed up or slow down.

We include a simple metronome for you on this book's audio web page. Just scan the QR code at the front of this book. The metronome is below the songs. Practicing with a metronome makes your music smoother and more fun!

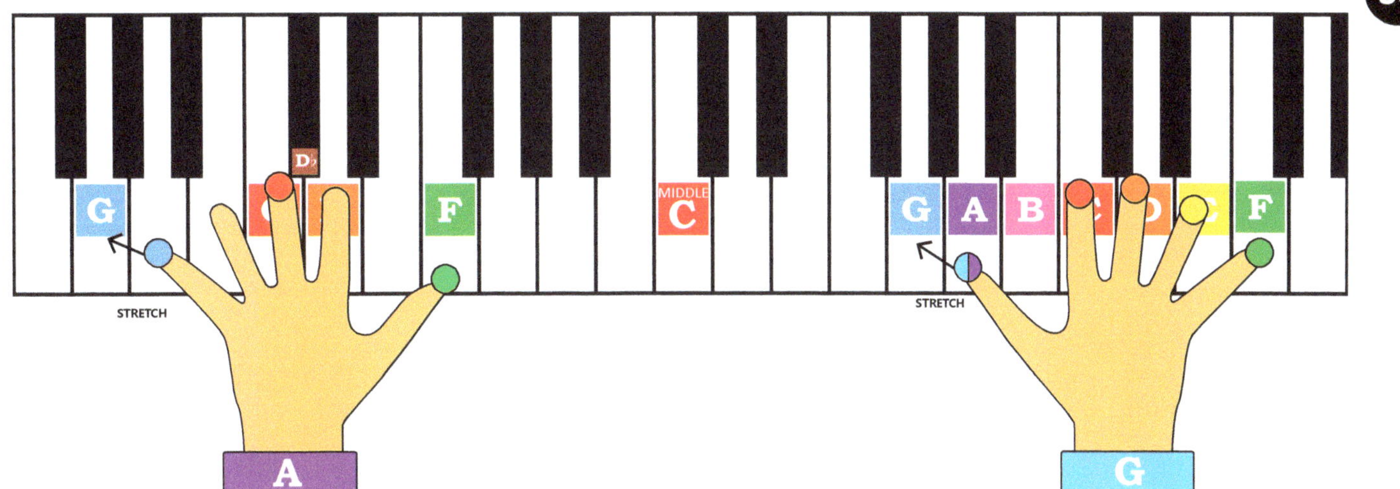

25. The Man on the Flying Trapeze

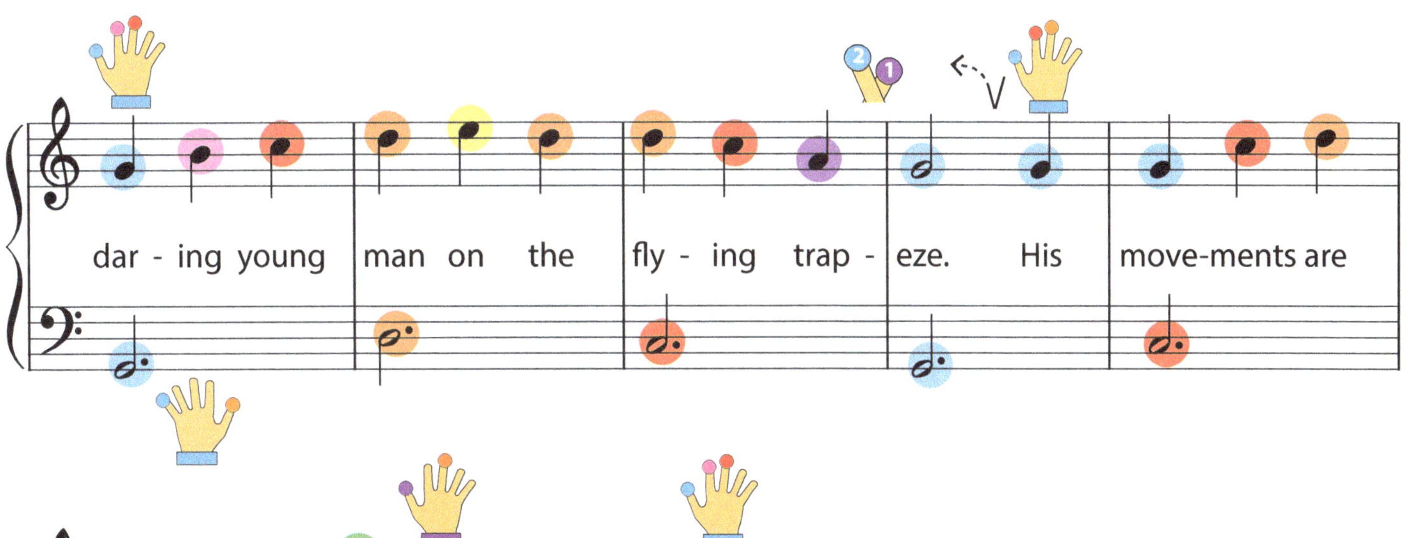

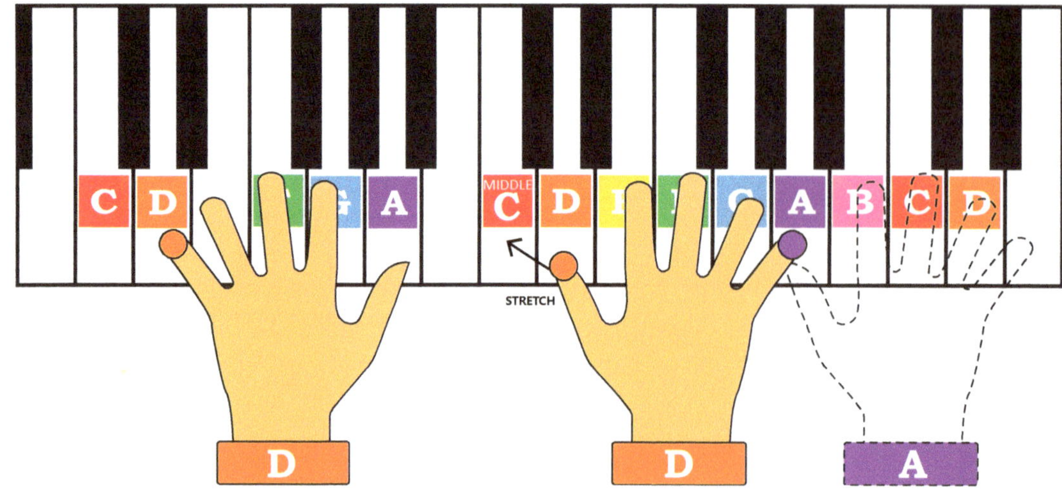

26. Drunken Sailor

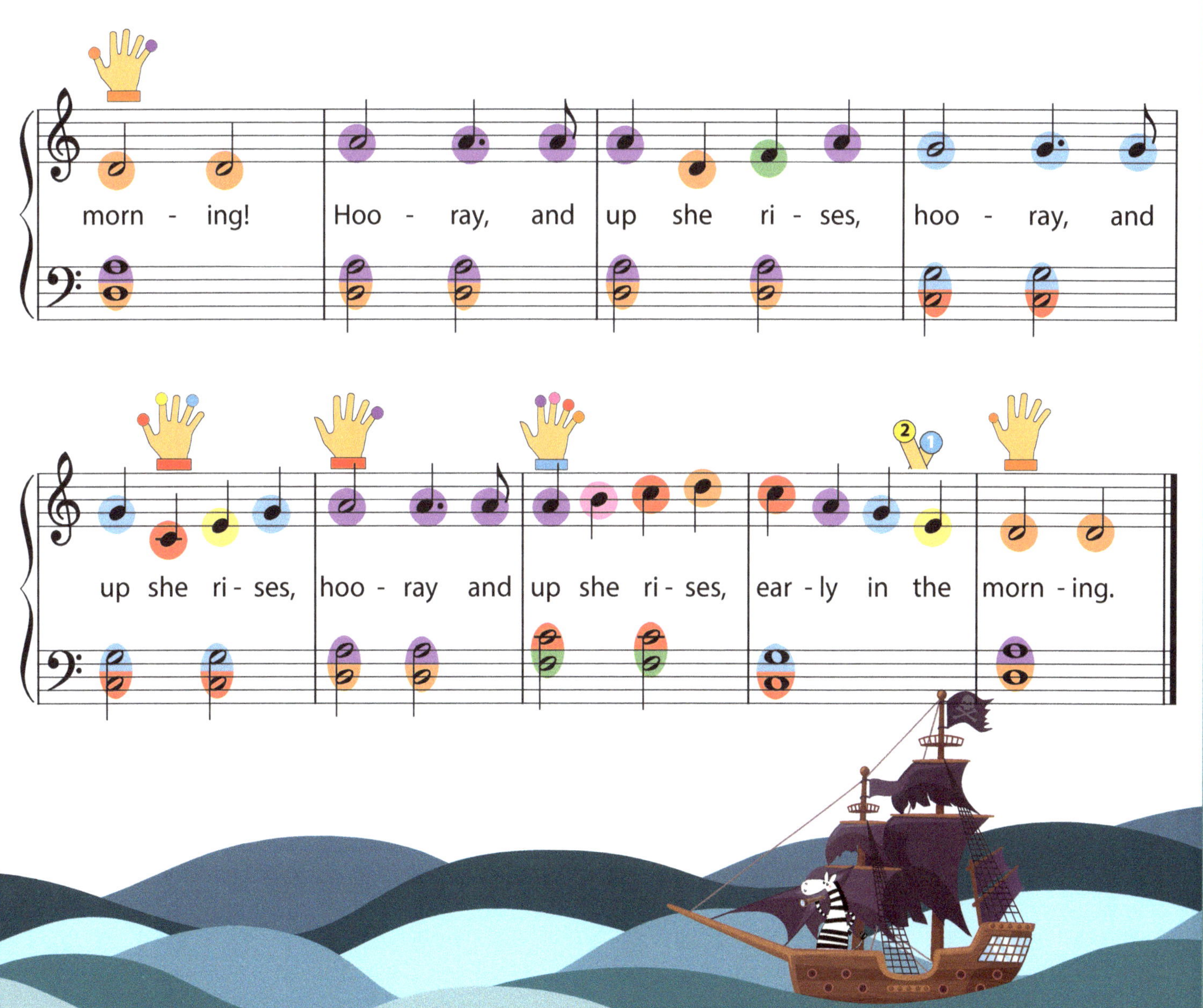
morn - ing!
Hoo - ray, and
up she ri - ses,
hoo - ray, and
up she ri - ses,
hoo - ray and
up she ri - ses,
ear - ly in the
morn - ing.
2
1

Exercise 7: Play the Chromatic Scale

Now that you've got some finger-walking experience, let's practice playing the full 12 notes, which includes the black-key half steps, with ease! This is called the chromatic scale.

Read the numbers above the notes to play with the correct finger.

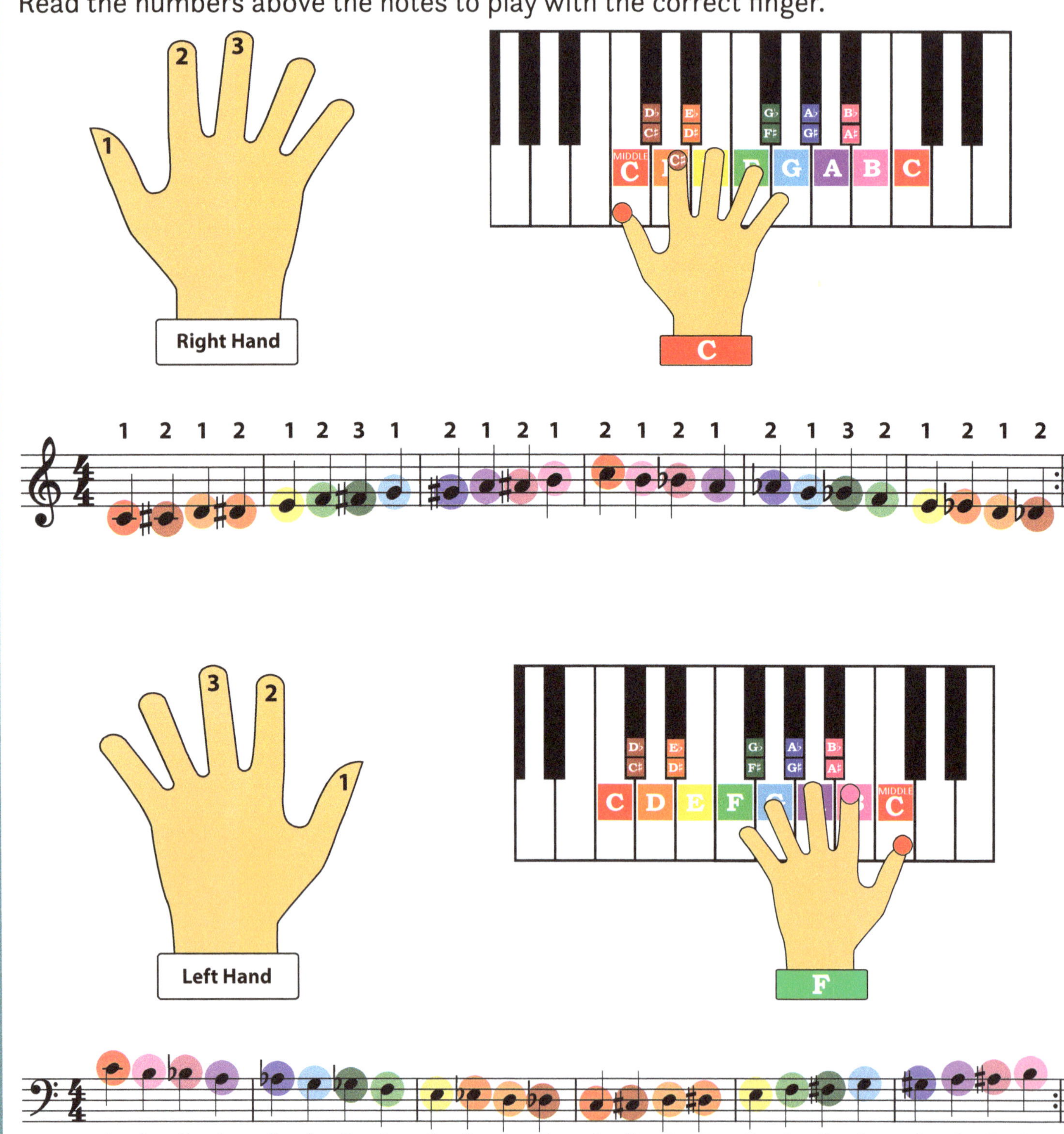

Chromatic Scale Challenge!

Can you play up and down your entire piano keyboard without stopping, or making a mistake?

Try with your right hand first, then your left. Alternate using your 2nd and 3rd fingers for the crossover.

The thumb should always play a white key. We've added the finger numbers below to help you. Follow the diagrams first. Once you have the hang of it, do the exercise without looking at the page!

Right Hand — Going up the Chromatic Scale

Left Hand — Going Down the Chromatic Scale

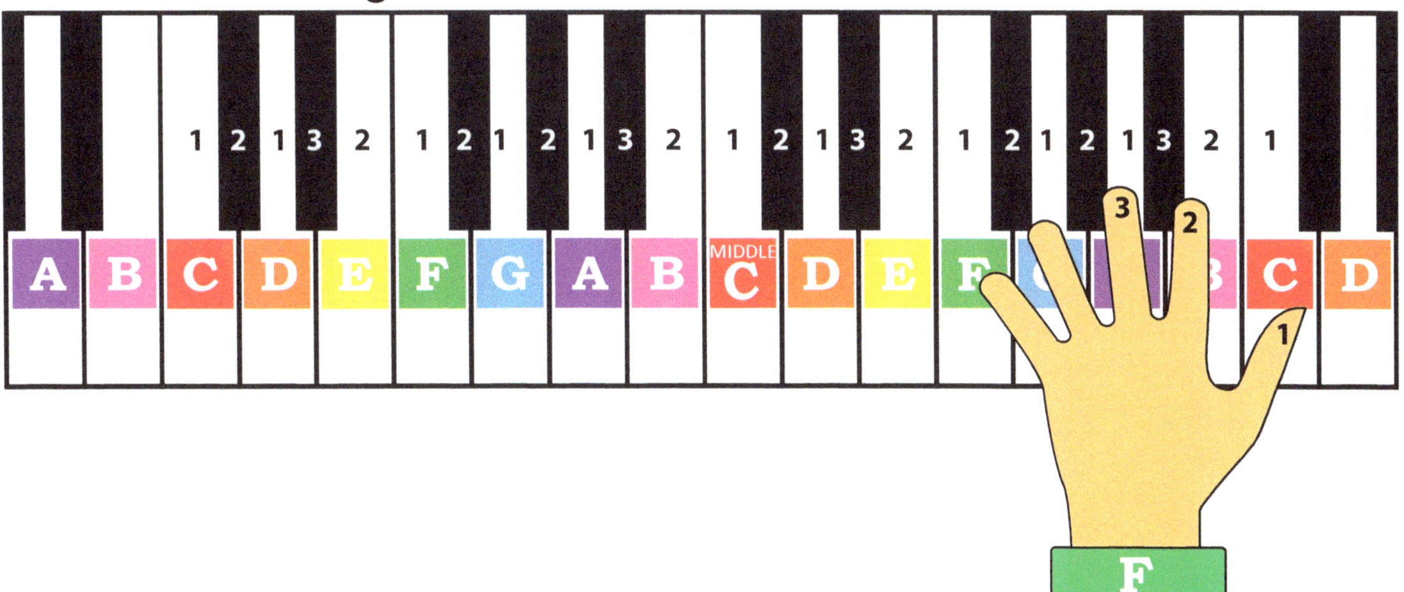

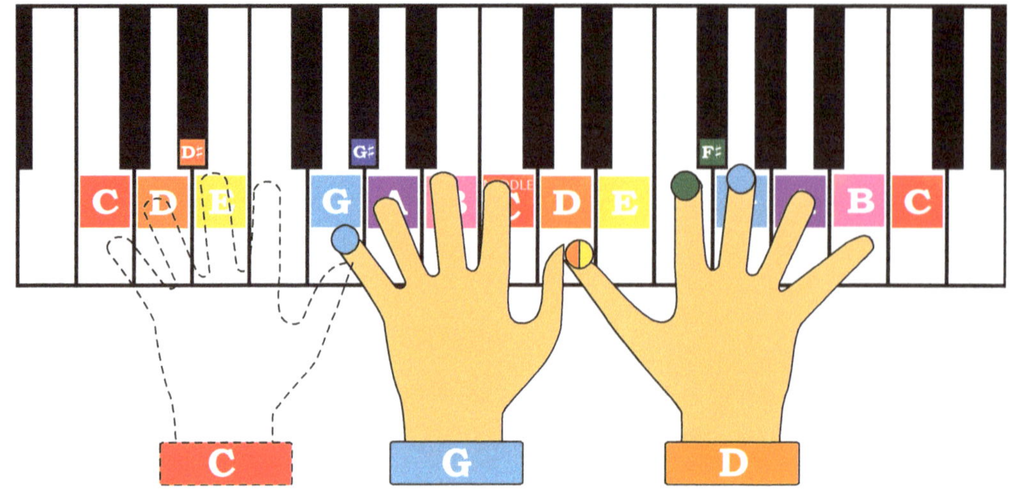
D♯
G♯
F♯
C
D
E
G
A
B
C
D
E
B
C
C
G
D

27. Aura Lea

27

As the black - bird
in the Spring,
'neath the wil - low
tree,

sat and piped, I
heard him sing,
sing - ing Au - ra
Lea.

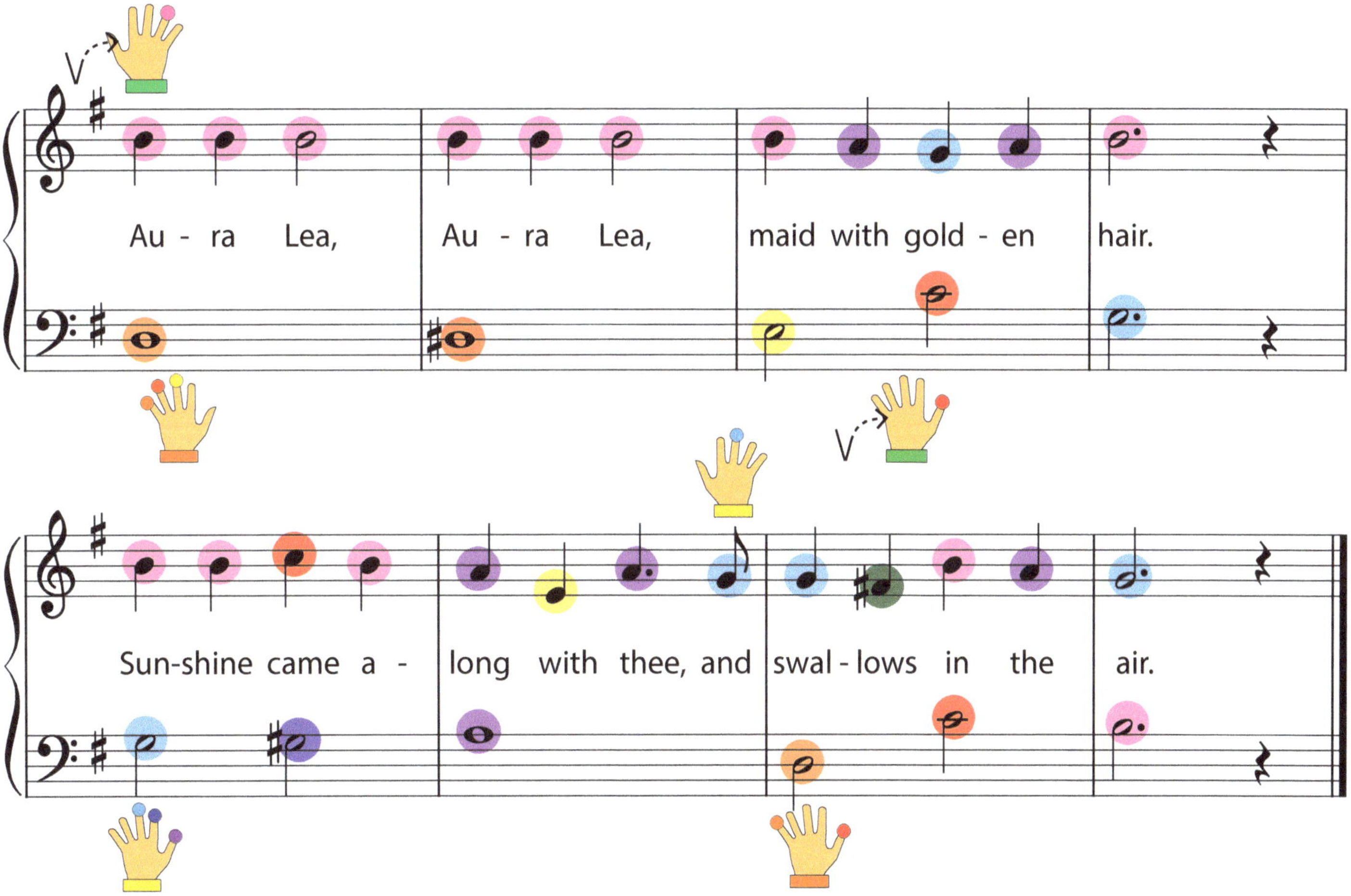

Au - ra Lea, Au - ra Lea, maid with gold - en hair.

Sun-shine came a - long with thee, and swal - lows in the air.

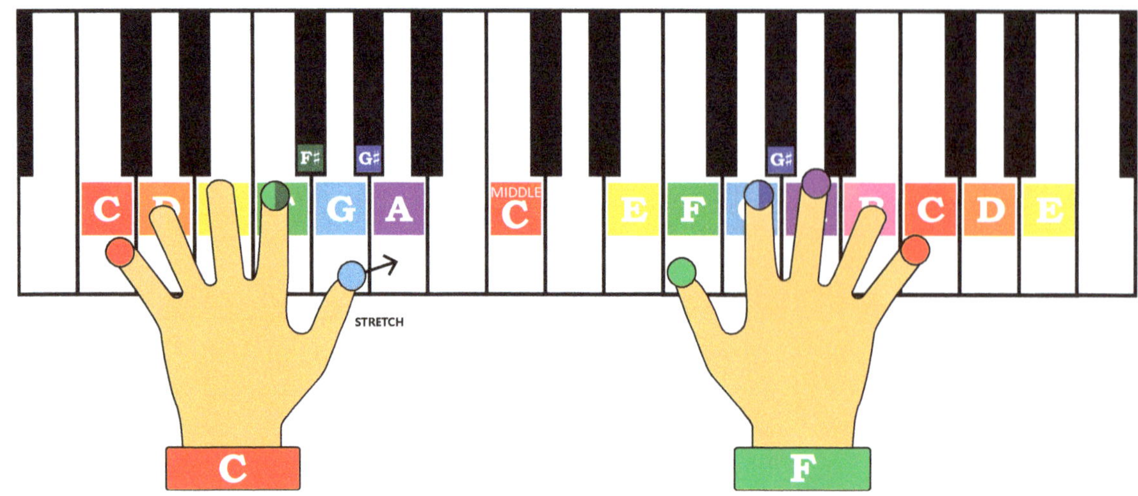

28. Sailing, Sailing

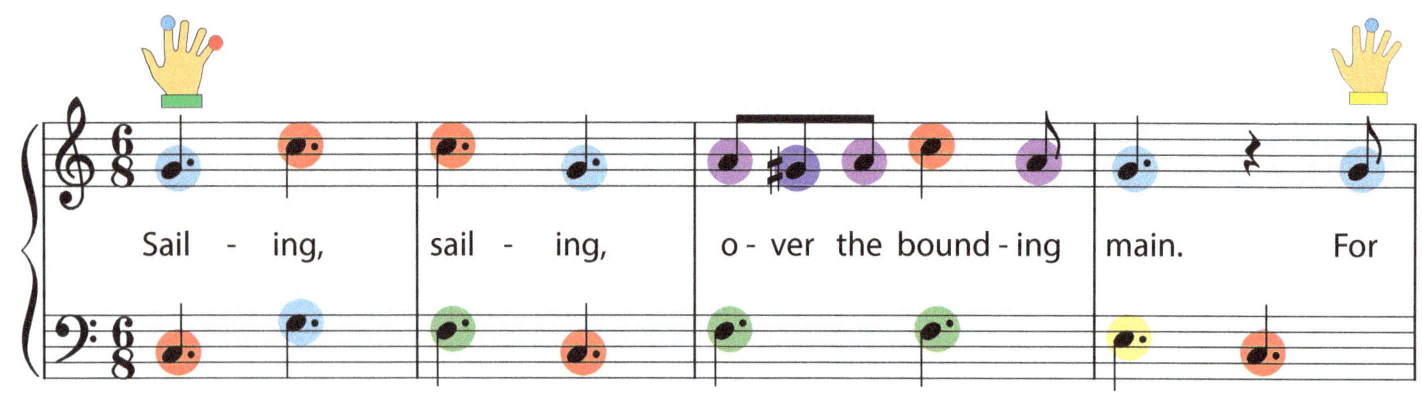

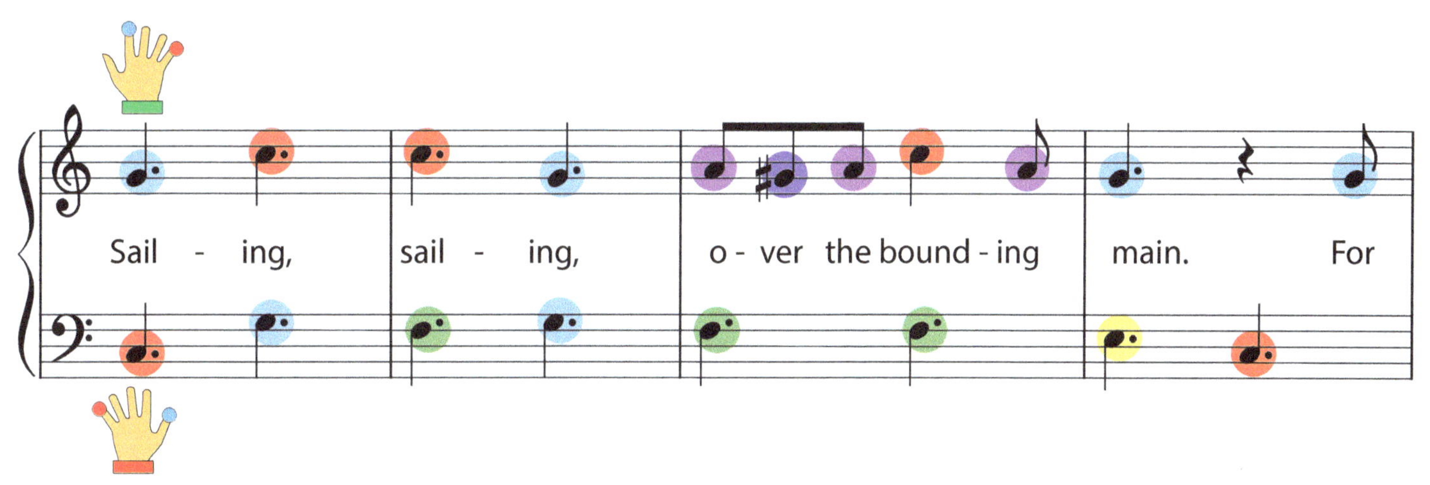
Sail - ing, sail - ing, o - ver the bound - ing main. For

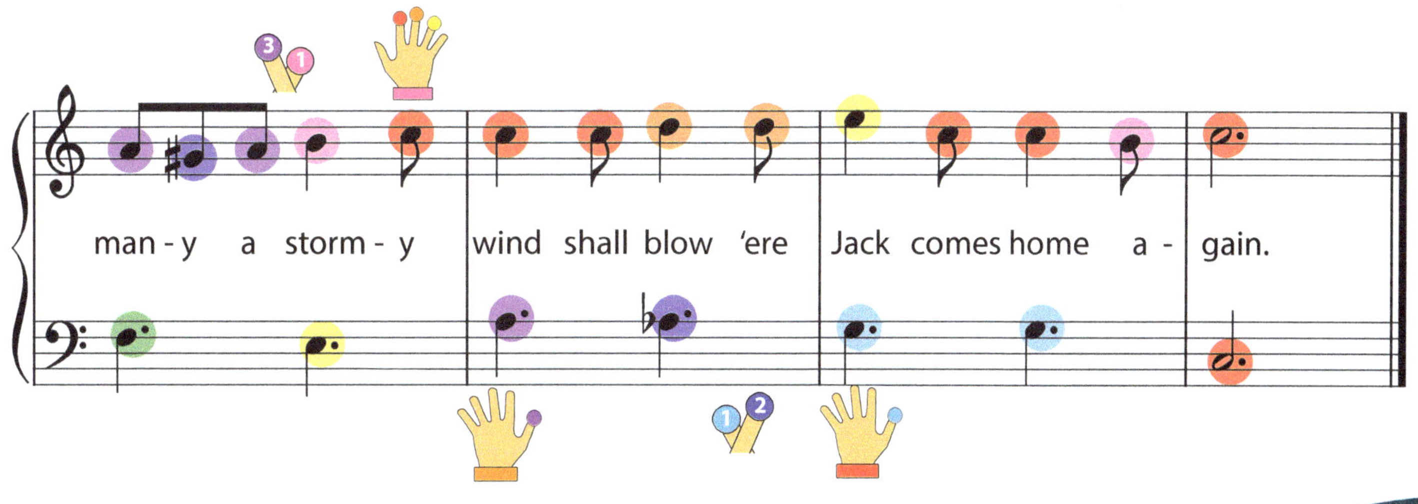
3
1
2
man - y a storm - y wind shall blow 'ere Jack comes home a - gain.

Exercise 8: Arpeggio Practice

Let's practice something a little more complicated—an arpeggio including a black key. Remember to keep your hands loose and flexible to reach all the keys you need. Be ready to move the hand forward and backward as needed.

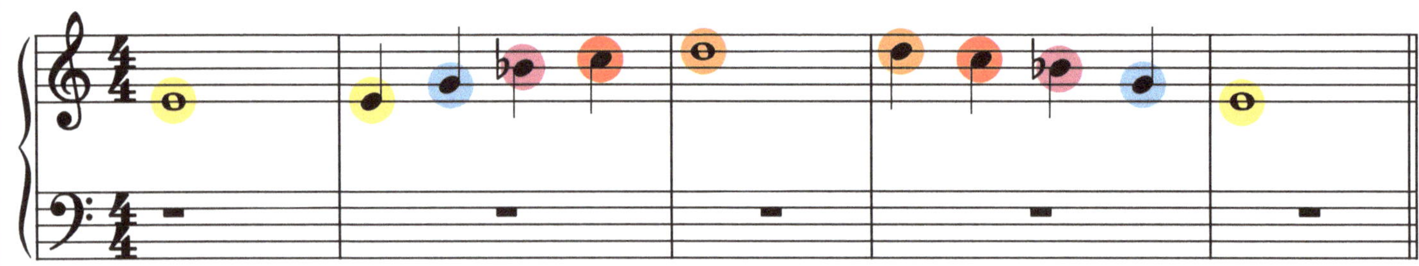

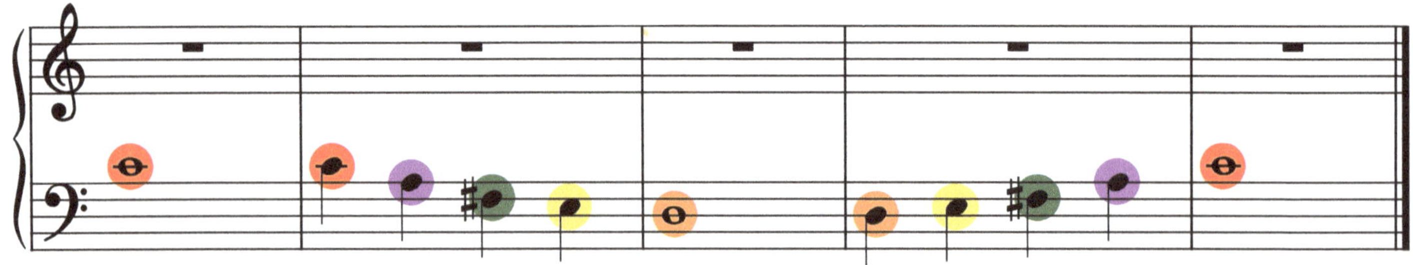

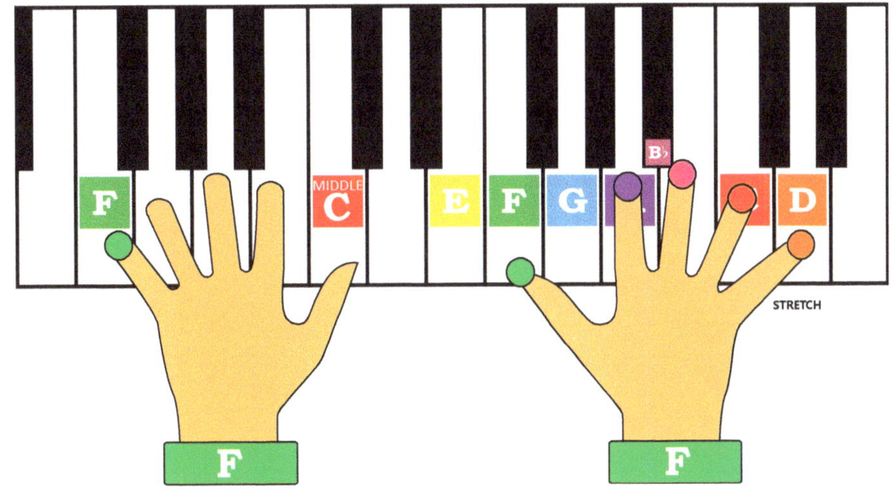

29. He's Got the Whole World in His Hands

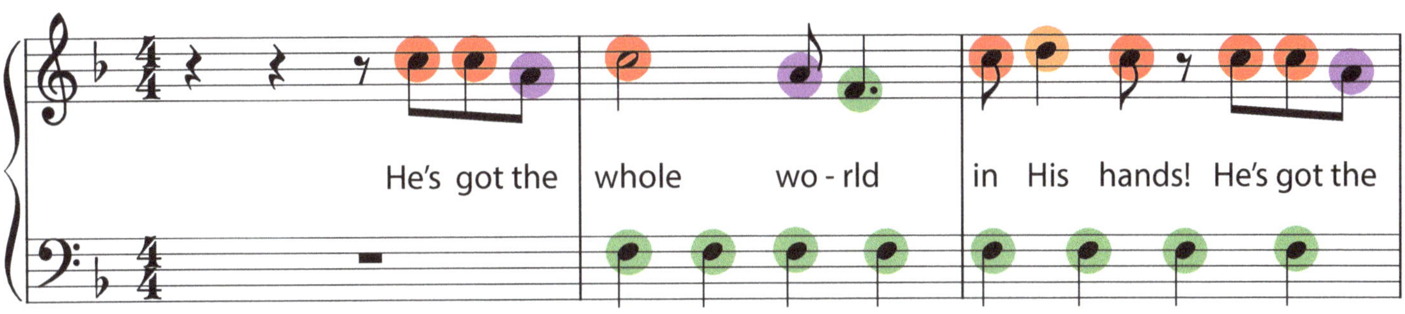

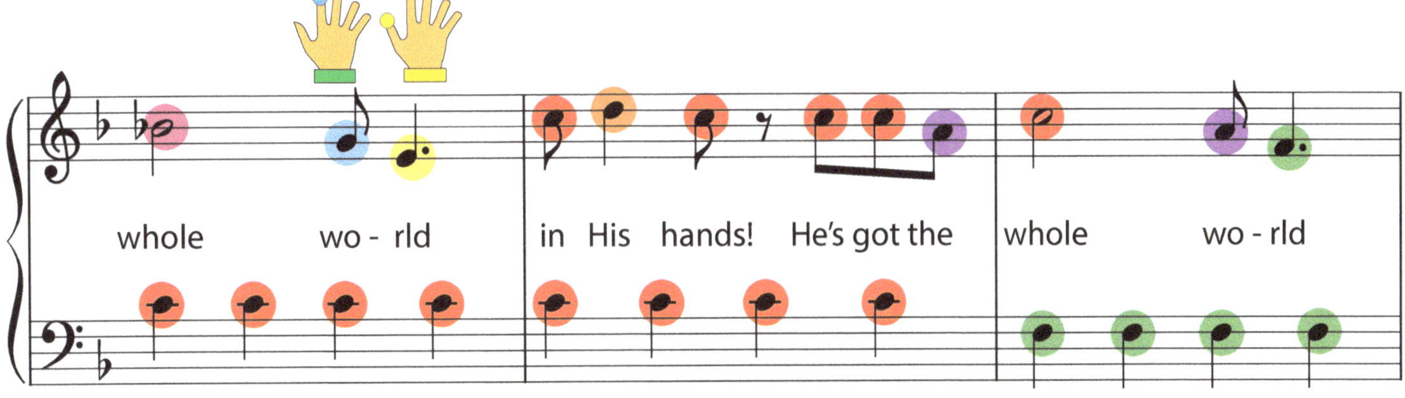

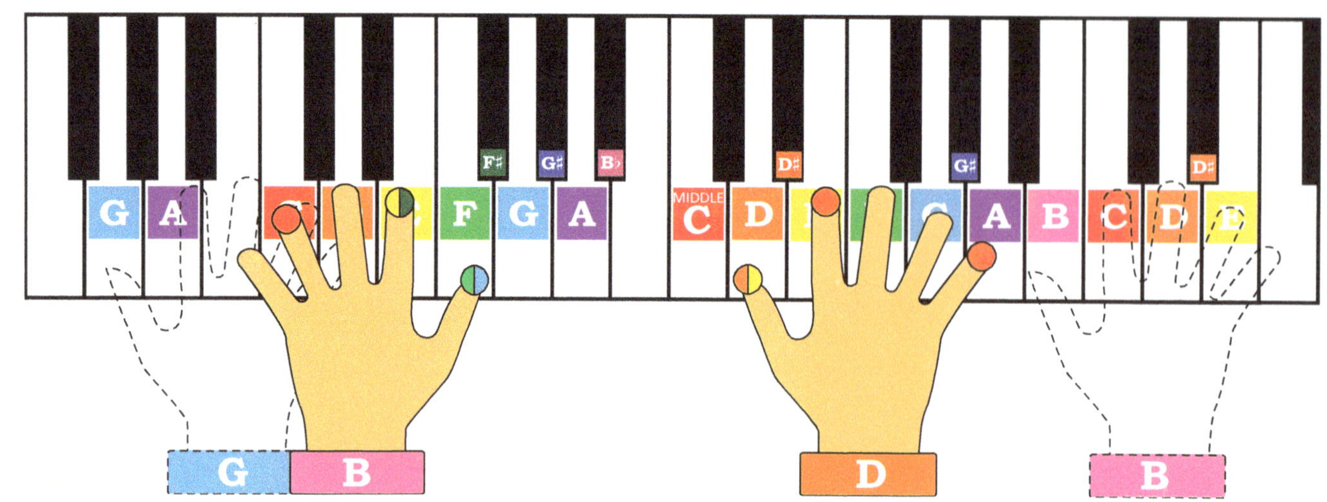

30. The Entertainer

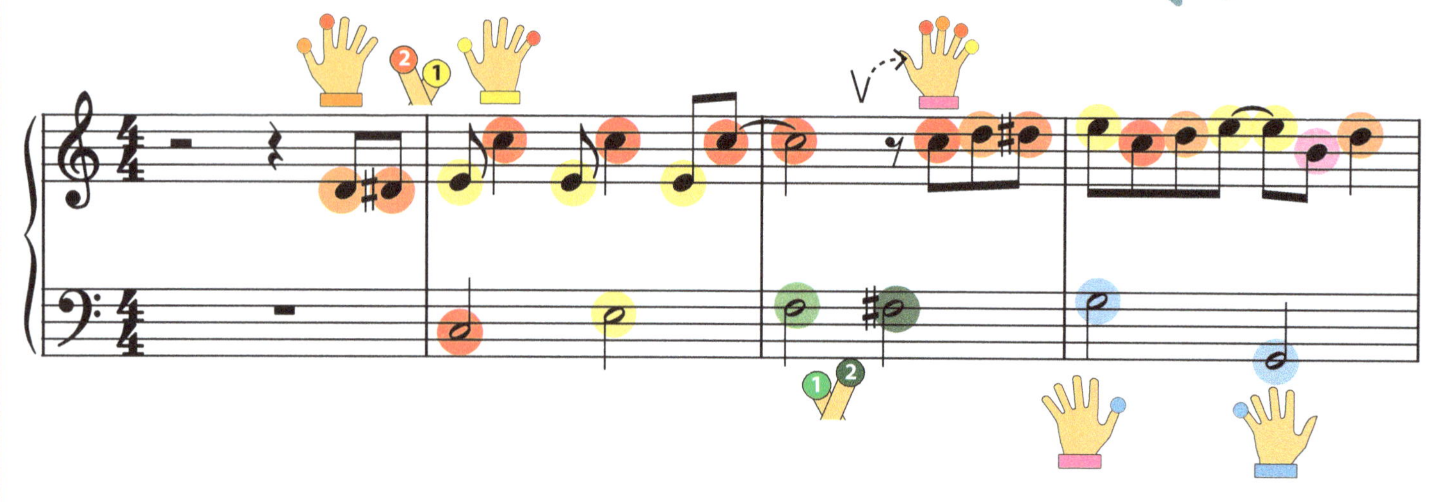

2
1
1
3
1
2
1
2

Tired of scissors and tape? Upgrade to our premium keyboard stickers. Specially designed to match this book perfectly, these sheets are available to purchase in your local currency at jenniferkemmeter.com/stickers or by scanning this QR code:

Cut the labels below and attach them to your piano keys as shown on page 8.

Standard size piano key labels

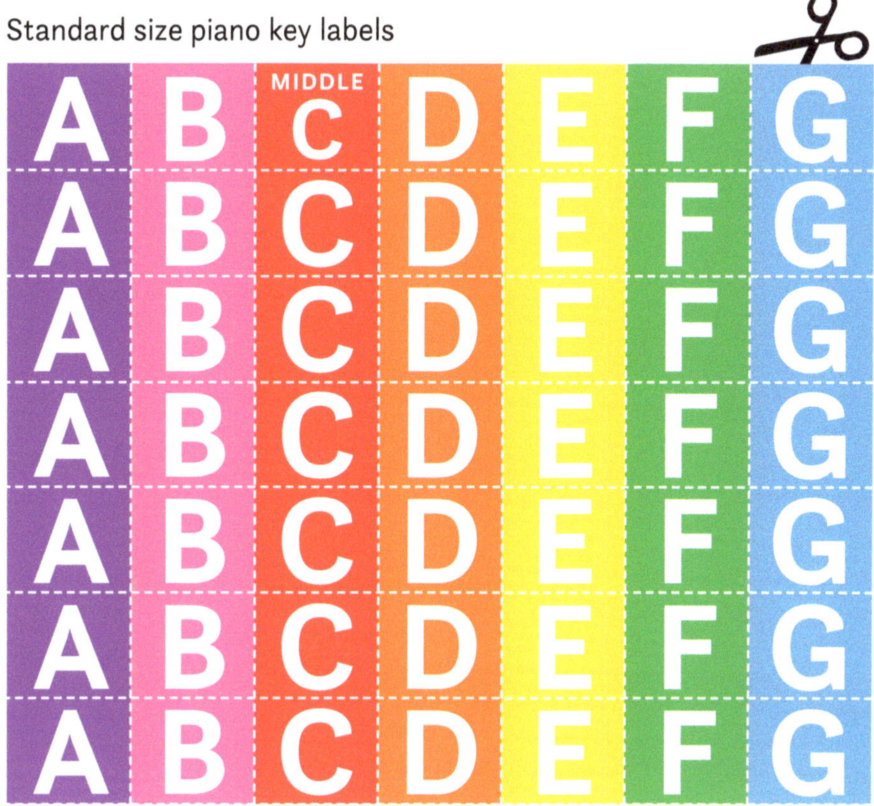

Mini key labels

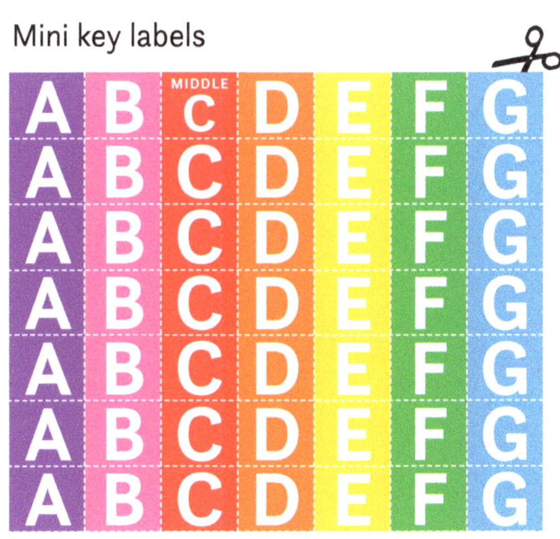

Mid-size piano key labels

Cut the labels below and attach them to your piano keys as shown on page 8.

Standard size piano key labels

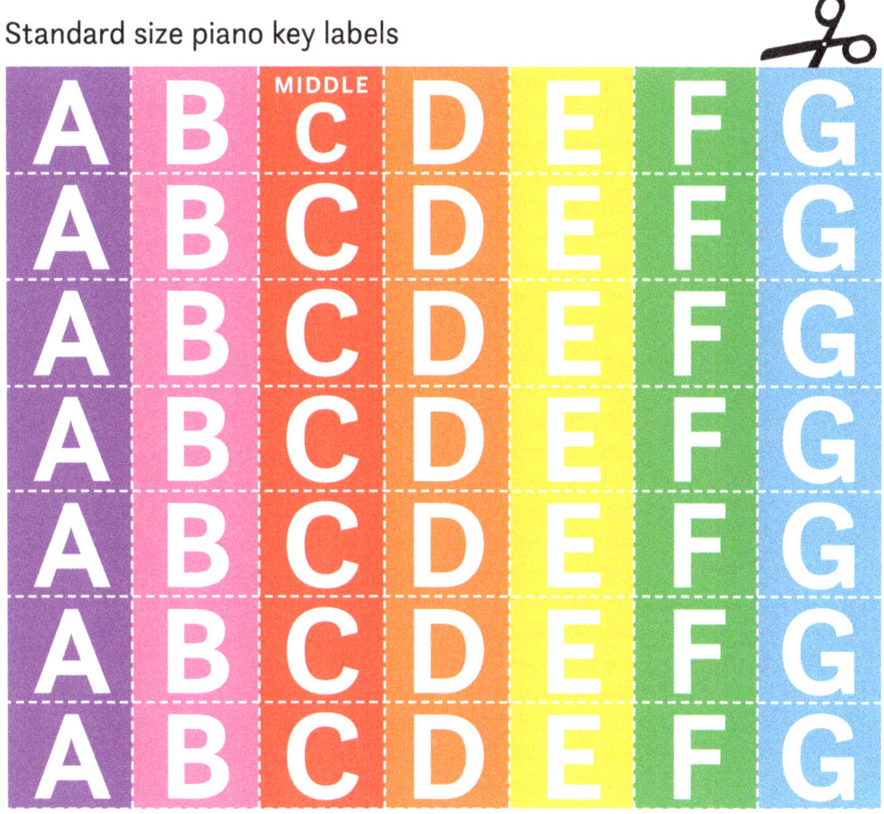

Mini key labels

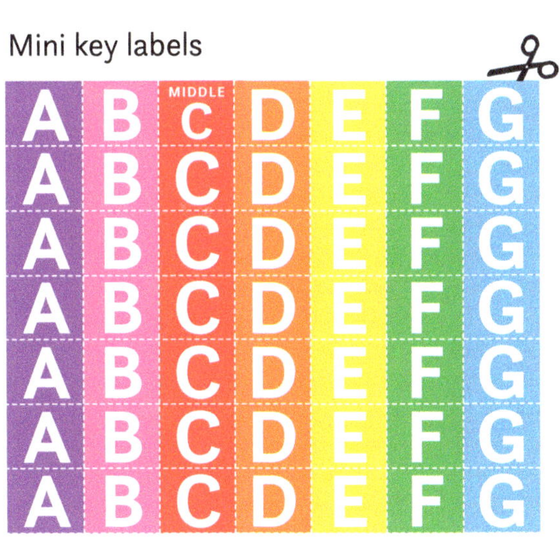

Mid-size piano key labels

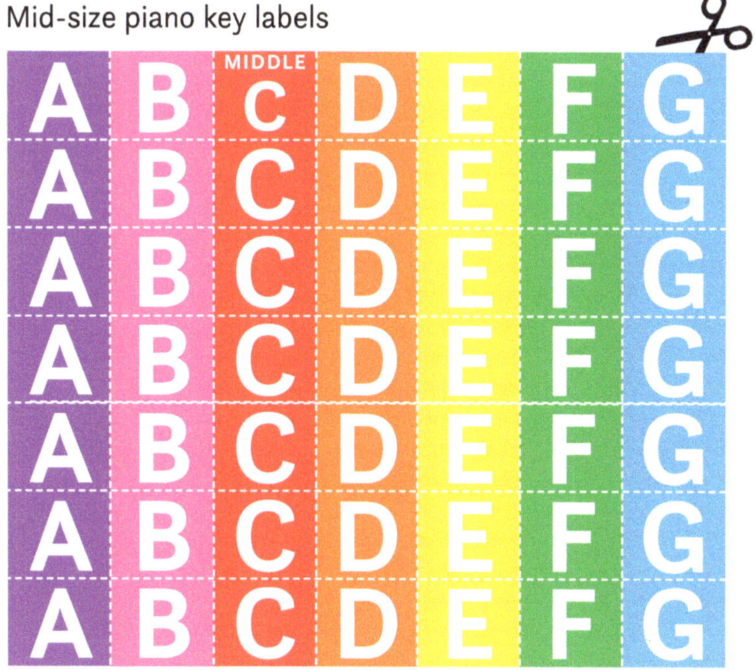

Congratulations!

____

(your name)

worked hard

and completed

Play It!

LEVEL 2

CHILDREN'S SONGS

www.ingramcontent.com/pod-product-compliance
Lightning Source LLC
LaVergne TN
LVHW060641110826
845147LV00018B/1021
9781513142029